e
pluribus
**ENGLISH**

**ALSO BY THE AUTHOR**

*Smart Words: Vocabulary for the Erudite
(and Those Who Wish to Be)*

*Wicked Good Words: From Johnnycakes to Jug Handles,
a Roundup of America's Regionalisms*

*Words at Work: An Insider's Guide to
the Language of Professions*

*A Short Biography of John F. Kennedy*

*A Short Biography of Jacqueline Kennedy*

# WORDS IN PRAISE OF MIM'S WORDS

### *E Pluribus English*

"Mim Harrison gives us a delightfully erudite romp through the English language, celebrating its riotous, border-crossing history with wit, warmth and a lexicographer's love of nuance. Revealing the hidden stories behind everyday words, she shows how this magpie of languages has borrowed, blended and blundered its way into the rich patchwork we speak today. A must-read for word lovers, language learners, and anyone who has ever wondered where we got words like 'galore' and 'kerfuffle'—and what 'glamour' has to do with 'grammar.'"
—Ross King, *New York Times* bestselling author of *Brunelleschi's Dome* and *The Bookseller of Florence*

"Wow! This book is such a fun and fantastic romp through the histories and hidden stories of both ordinary and odd words of English. Delights await on every page. And of course, the word 'page' comes from the Latin *pangere*, which meant to fasten. I find that fasten-ating, which we now spell as "fascinating," and say that of any book that fastens itself, like this one, page after page to your heart and mind. Get it for your own enjoyment, and give it to your friends. They will love it and you for bringing it to them."
—Tom Morris, PhD, bestselling author of such books as *True Success*, *If Aristotle Ran General Motors*, *The Oasis Within*, and *Philosophy for Dummies*

"*E Pluribus English* is wicked good! Mim Harrison takes us on a wonderful journey across time and place that enlightens us about the story of English with charm, wit, and perspective. I read her book with so many aha and laugh-aloud moments, and applaud her ultimate message to relish English and be open to where it can take us."
—Lorie Roule, Senior Executive at Transparent Language, Inc.

## *Words at Work*

"A treat for word addicts like me."
—ROBERT MACNEIL, co-author of *The Story of English*

"It will help you sound like an insider."
—CHICAGO TRIBUNE

"*Words at Work* collects some of the best insider language from common professions."
—THE SEATTLE TIMES

## *Smart Words*

"If you've ever wished for snazzier words to clothe your thoughts, *Smart Words* is a bottomless wardrobe of elegant and sophisticated options."
—ERIN MCKEAN, Editor, *VERBATIM: The Language Quarterly*

"Mim Harrison puts powerful, evocative words in your vocabulary as she asks her reader: why merely criticize when you can castigate, or why be indirect when you can be circuitous?"
—PAUL DICKSON, author of *Family Words: A Dictionary of the Secret Language of Families*

## *Wicked Good Words*

"A fascinating survey of idioms."
—ST. PETERSBURG TIMES

"Simultaneously full of witty asides and linguistic erudition, *Wicked Good Words* is one of those rare books that you will read too fast and will find yourself wishing you could read for the first time all over again."
—AMMON SHEA, author of *Reading the OED*

e
pluribus
# ENGLISH

The many languages we speak
when we speak English

## MIM HARRISON

Published by America the Bilingual Press
420 South Congress Avenue
Delray Beach, Florida USA
www.americathebilingual.com

Copyright © 2025 Mim Harrison. All rights reserved.
ISBN: 978-1-7339375-6-6
Library of Congress Control Number: 2025915587

America the Bilingual is a project of the Levenger Foundation, which supports bilingualism and biliteracy in the Americas.

Cover and interior design by
Tabitha Lahr, www.tabithalahrdesign.com

Cover image © iStockphoto.com
Interior vine illustration © Shutterstock.com
Author's photo by Denise

*For Cami and Sofi.*

*When your mother would teasingly ask, "Where are my princesses?," I always knew: right here, forever in my heart.*

*Unlocking the English language will become equivalent to rebuilding the Tower of Babel.*
—Harold Bloom


*The development of English has always been more a matter of structured chaos than anything that we might call logic.*
—John McWhorter

 **MEANDERTHAL,** *n.* One whose ideas meander, diverge, digress, detour, and occasionally just fall off the cliff onto tangents. One who ponders, in other words, the English language.

# CONTENTS

Of Legends and Vines........................................ xii

## First Thoughts

1. To *'Foreign,'* Let Us Say: *'Fooey'*........................ 1

## Part One: The Pond, East

2. Speak Like a Proto-Indo-European with
   These Ten Easy Terms!.................................... 7
3. The Earliest English Wasn't English at All................ 13
4. The English Is Coming! The English Is Coming!............ 23
5. Bless Those Romans, They Finally Got Religion............ 31
6. Comes a Norseman: Vikings Take Loot, Leave Language..... 39
7. What the Englisc Called Arabisc........................... 47
8. It's Greek to ... Well, Just About Everybody.............. 57
9. Bonjour, Bayeux: English Channels French................. 69
10. Why Can't the English Teach Their
    Children How to Spell?................................... 79
11. Romancing the Renaissance............................... 87
12. No Academy, Please: It's English........................ 101
13. The Empire Strikes...................................... 111

## Part Two: The Pond, West

14. *Mabrīka* to America . . . . . . . . . . . . . . . . . . . . . . 123
15. Side-by-Side-by-Spanish . . . . . . . . . . . . . . . . . . . 139
16. And the Grammy Goes to . . . Gullah! . . . . . . . . . . . 151
17. Beignets, Grief Bacon, and Bagels . . . . . . . . . . . . . 163
18. "A Language Cannot Be Too Rich" . . . . . . . . . . . . . 179

## Last Words (for Now)

19. Bilenglish, or: What Language Can You Speak When You Speak English? . . . . . . . . . . . . . . . . . . 189

Bibliography . . . . . . . . . . . . . . . . . . . . . . . . . . . . . 194
Acknowledgments . . . . . . . . . . . . . . . . . . . . . . . . . 227
Index of Words . . . . . . . . . . . . . . . . . . . . . . . . . . . 229
About the Author . . . . . . . . . . . . . . . . . . . . . . . . . . 235

# OF LEGENDS AND VINES

## Language Legend

If you're curious about the language names that appear on the cover, here's a cheat sheet for you.

| | |
|---|---|
| al-ʿarabiyyah | Arabic |
| Ceilteach | Celtic |
| Deutsch | German |
| elakómkwik* | Algonquian |
| Elliniká | Greek |
| español | Spanish |
| eydish | Yiddish |
| fornnorræna | Old Norse |
| français | French |
| Gullah | Gullah |
| Hindi | Hindi |
| Latinus | Latin |
| Nāhuatl | Nahuatl |
| Nederlands | Dutch |
| Nihongo | Japanese |
| Qheswa simi | Quechua |
| saṃskṛta | Sanskrit |
| Taíno | Taíno |

---

\* The word, which means "they are our relatives/allies," has been used to describe the Algonquins.

Impressive as this list may be, it's not the last word on all the languages that make up English. Chinese, Portuguese, and Tagalog also make an appearance in the book. And even more make an appearance on English-speaking tongues.

In some instances, what you're seeing in this legend is a transliteration: the name of the language is presented in the Roman (Latin) alphabet rather than its own. (Elliniká, for example, in the Greek alphabet is ελληνικά.) To borrow a bit of that Latin, the modus operandi was clarity and consistency, with a minimum of head-scratching on your part. "Elliniká," after all, isn't that far from "Hellenic," so you may have even guessed it meant Greek. As the Greeks are fond of saying, *Bravo!*

## The Vignettes

Each chapter in Parts One and Two concludes with a series of vignettes—primarily, examples of words that entwined around English from the language we explore in the chapter. *Vignette* originally referred to the decorative border, resembling a vine, found in some illustrated manuscripts and books.

Is anyone surprised that **vignette** is from the French, as it trails back to *vigne*, meaning vineyard? Consider the vignettes in these chapters as small stories that you savor through the grapevine. *Santé!*

# FIRST THOUGHTS

## 1.
## TO 'FOREIGN,'
## LET US SAY: 'FOOEY'†

I have long had a loathe affair with the word "foreign." It began, not surprisingly, when I was branded such, as an American college student spending a junior year abroad in England. As I made my way to the local police station shortly after arriving to register my whereabouts, the person in charge crisply informed me that "we like to keep track of you foreigners."

Ouch.

I was being labeled an outsider: **foreign** stems from the Latin *foris,* for outside. A stranger. Someone who didn't belong. Someone for whom "alien" always hovered menacingly close (and landed on my English husband who, when he resided in the US before he was eligible for citizenship, was classified as a "resident alien").

The *Online Etymology Dictionary* also sees a connection between *foreign* and *forest,* a place that can be downright scary if you get lost in it. Just ask Hansel and Gretel. And notice how close the Italian word for "foreigner" is: *forestiero.*

With a language that has as many words as English does—upwards of 171,000 currently serving active duty in the *Oxford English Dictionary*—surely we can come up with one less fraught and unfriendly than "foreign." Only the Veterans of Foreign Wars should lay claim to it.

(As for "alien," the Library of Congress struck it from its topic headings in 2021, replacing it with "noncitizen.")

Why do we engage in *foreign* relations with countries when we're trying to find common ground? (Thesaurus alternative: international.) And why, in too many instances, do we refer to languages other than our own as *foreign*? (Thesaurus again: global, world.)

Besides, you could argue that if any language should be considered "foreign," it's English.

To varying degrees, English is: Celtic, Germanic, Scandinavian, Latin, French, Greek, Arabic, Hindi, Dutch, and Spanish. In America, add influences of African and Indigenous languages as well, together with Yiddish.

So, given how many other languages come spilling out of our mouths every day, if anyone should not view other languages as "foreign," it's us native-English speakers. If ever there were a gateway drug for enjoying other languages, ours is surely it.

When we view our language from this vantage point, we might come to feel more at home with other languages, especially those that are not really strangers to our tongue. We might even try speaking one of them.

So what's holding us back?

## The problem with English

For starters, only recently has there been enough of an impetus for native-English speakers to branch out linguistically. After all, about 1.35 billion people on Earth speak English. Almost anywhere we are in the world, we're likely to bump into one of them.

But as Steve Leveen, a champion of American bilingualism, tells us in his book, *America's Bilingual Century,* there are now many reasons for us to venture beyond our linguistic border. Some of these reasons are practical, given the global nature of business, science, and other professions today. And some are personal, as when Steve persuades us to "live your larger life by living part of it in another language, enjoying the expanded experiences that bilingualism brings."

And yet, at least two well-regarded linguists point out the major challenge that native-English speakers face when trying to learn another language. (Not those young kids, with their little sponge brains, but the rest of us.)

"English speakers do not have any language that is sufficiently close to English that it can be picked up easily," says Professor John McWhorter of Columbia University, in *The Story of Human Language,* one of his many guides and books on the language.

Gaston Dorren, the Dutch polyglot, linguist, and author of *Lingo* and *Babel*, agrees. He points to the "massive borrowing" that goes on in English that makes it such a deviant. "Being a native English speaker has a raft of advantages," he writes in *Babel*, " . . . but it does have this major drawback. Most English speakers are severely monolingual."

Ah, now there's a gauntlet just begging to be picked up.

Not to disagree with these leading linguists, but maybe, just as with "foreign," we should approach this seemingly innate weakness a different way.

## Obstacles as impetus

Perhaps the "massive borrowing" that English does so well has a flip side. Maybe since English has the capacity to absorb so many languages, it's also possible that those of us who speak it can absorb *something* from other languages, too. After all, the **sofa** you sit on is from Arabic; the **courtesy** you extend someone is French; the **panic** you might feel is Greek. And on it goes for all of the languages in English's borrow bag, as we shall see. (Most of the boldfaced words you come upon are in the index, fyi.)

Another way to psych ourselves up for learning another language is to indulge in a little **schadenfreude.** (There: we just added German.)

The Oxford Royale Academy has a long list of infractions against logic that English commits, making it hard for second-language learners to learn it. They include, but are not limited to: exceptions to the rules of grammar; godawful spelling; pronunciation that can be confusing (see spelling); homophones that run rampant—cell and sell, flour and flower, core and corps. Other language sites cite similar grievances. (Site and cite: rack up another one.)

You can take some consolation, then, in the fact that, while English is widely held to be a difficult language for non-native speakers to master, *you* already have. But that's not to lord it over non-native speakers. ("Lord over" is the kind of idiom that also adds to the list of grievances, by the way.) It's to give yourself a pep talk.

There's one more arrow we native speakers have in our quiver when it comes to taking on, and taking in, another language. It's one that we word nerds can brandish, and it's potent: being word lovers makes us wonder how all these English words came to be. That interest in their etymology takes us places, linguistically speaking.

For me, learning Latin and French in school, and now attempting Spanish years later, gives me a greater appreciation for English because of the ways these languages have enriched it. But the inverse is also true.

The more I learn about the languages that created English, the more interested I become in them. And it's not just about words that are comparable in English. I finally was able to remember all the days of the week in Spanish when I learned that most of them are name derivatives of the planets. Their etymology, in other words.

Then came the eye-opening day when I discovered it was no coincidence that the Spanish *ojalá* sounded uncannily like the Arabic *inshalla*. Not only that, but the two had a comparable meaning of "hopefully." And so, of course, I had to find out why . . . which led me to more words in Spanish that were birthed in Arabic. (See chapter 7.)

I credit English for this discovery because, thanks to its history, it's a language capable of sparking great curiosity in other languages. And it's a reminder that there's no such thing as a *foreign* language, just a language we don't know.

That's why exploring the many languages we speak when we speak English matters. Even if we won't know all or even most of another language, we can try to acquire enough of it so that it becomes something familiar and fun, rather than formidable and forbidding. *Ojalá*, it could be the start of a brand new language awakening—and who knows what adventures await?

So come, join me in this meanderthalling, and witness how this mashup called English serves as a lively ambassador of the wonder and delights found in many of the world's languages.

---

† Why *fooey* and not *phooey*? See chapter 10, "Why Can't the English Teach Their Children How to Spell?"

# PART ONE:
# THE POND, EAST

"No critic and advocate of immutability has ever once managed properly or even marginally to outwit the English language's capacity for foxy and relentlessly slippery flexibility...."
—Simon Winchester,
*The Meaning of Everything:
The Story of the Oxford English Dictionary*

# 2.
# SPEAK LIKE A PROTO-INDO-EUROPEAN WITH THESE TEN EASY TERMS!

"Speak the speech, I pray you, as I pronounc'd it to you, trippingly on the tongue," instructs Shakespeare's Hamlet jauntily. But just what speech are you speaking when you speak English, and how many tongues might you be tripping on?

Before there was English—or Celtic, or German or French, or even Latin and Sanskrit—there was a language dating back approximately seven thousand years ascribed to early peoples of what is now eastern Europe. We know it as Proto-Indo-European, or PIE. Hardly a catchy name for a language, but it's a helpful corral for doing the linguistic equivalent of herding cats, as it brings together a group of seemingly disparate languages.

Think of PIE as a massive tree with lots of branches. Or a large family flung far and wide in unexpected ways.

## The PIE of many pieces

An Englishman named William Jones deserves much of the credit for first recognizing uncanny similarities among different languages. His discovery dates to around 1786, spurred on by England's presence in India, where Jones worked in the judicial courts. He was fascinated with Indian culture, including its language. And then he noticed something: Sanskrit was similar in some ways to both Latin and Greek (both of which he knew, in addition to a congeries of other languages). He described it like this:

> The *Sanscrit* language, whatever be its antiquity, is of a wonderful structure; more perfect than the *Greek*, more copious than the *Latin*, and more exquisitely refined than either, yet bearing to both of them a stronger affinity, both in the roots of verbs and the forms of grammar, than could possibly have been produced by accident; so strong indeed, that no philologer could examine them all three, without believing them to have sprung from some common source, which, perhaps, no longer exists.

And thus *father* in English evokes *pater* in Latin, which in turn echoes *pitar* in Sanskrit.

Jacob Grimm, of the famous Grimm brothers' fairy tales, later corroborated Jones's theory, adding Germanic languages to the PIE. Germanic, Italic, and Celtic are major language groups that made their way at various times in history, and in various tongues, to what we now call England. They are among the dozens of language families that made up this ancient PIE.

In his *Wall Street Journal* review of Laura Spinney's *Proto,* an exploration of just how far-reaching this PIE was, Michael Patrick Brady cites her observation that "[t]he most successful language the world ever knew was a hybrid trafficked by migrants." English, Brady points out, has a comparable story: an ever-unfolding language that's picked up all kinds of new perspectives along the way.

## Now for Those Easy Ten

Here are ten terms in PIE that are simple to connect to English. You'll also see how similar some of these terms are in other languages. The asterisk preceding each indicates that the word is, in linguistic parlance, "not attested." In other words, it's reconstructed. There is no written source, so the word has been inferred from the other terms it spawned.

| This in PIE . . . | . . . led to this in English |
|---|---|
| 1. *tu | **thou** (in Persian, *to* and in Celtic, *tū*) |
| 2. *septm̥ | **seven** (in Celtic, *secht* and in Sanskrit, *heptá*) |
| 3. *ĝénu | **knee** (in Latin, *genu* is knee—thus *genuflect*, bend the knee) |
| 4. *nas | **nose** (in Sanskrit, *nas*) |
| 5. *eḱwos | **equine**, from the Latin *equus* |
| 6. *kwon- | **dog**, from what grew to *canis* in Latin and *hund* in Old English |
| 7. *meli-t | **mellifluous**—which derived from the Latin *mel*, meaning honey (in Greek, *méli* and in Celtic, *mêl*); "mellifluous" describes something that's smooth as honey |
| 8. *gel- | **gelato**, which English welcomed from Italian; the PIE term meant "to freeze" |

| This in PIE . . . | . . . led to this in English |
|---|---|
| 9. *upér | **over,** which evolved from the Latin *super* (in Greek, *hupér*), which also combined with *stare*, meaning to stand—this led to **superstition,** an evolution that remains tantalizingly elusive (want to take up this gauntlet?) |
| 10. *sen- | **old;** in Latin, *senilis* |

## Senior Moment, Senate-Style

Okay, so *\*sen-* takes us to "old." As in **senile, senescence, senior.** Got it. But here comes the outlier, courtesy of ancient Rome's form of governance: **senate.**

The Roman Senate was a powerful advisory body. A respectful way of describing it would be as a council of elders (*senex* in Latin). The cheeky way would be as a bunch of old guys, which happens to also be correct.

The Romans believed that both wisdom and the accumulation of useful knowledge, qualities they valued, came with age. To be one who held these traits—a senator—was to hold a lofty place in the world. The formation of the US Senate was an idea that borrowed heavily from the Romans.

 **Meanderthal moment:** Not to be outdone in the old-guy department, the Greeks gave us *presbyteros*, and there's no coincidence it sounds like **Presbyterian.** *Presbyteros* means "priest" and is rooted in *presbys*, or old.

## 'Mom, Wood You Like Some Wine?'

The wine called **Madeira** takes its name from the island where it's produced. An autonomous Portuguese island off the coast of Morocco, Madeira in turn takes *its* name from the Portuguese word for **wood:** when Portugal's explorers came upon the island in the fifteenth century, they were struck by how heavily forested it was.

"Wood" derives from the Latin *materia* (timber), which in turn comes from PIE's *mater*. Yes, "mother," but in the fuller sense of the word: "origin," "source."

**A tree tangent this inspired:** Speaking of wood, can you guess the word that can trace its roots (pun intended) to a tree trunk? Consider how trees are often cut down to their trunks. That act of cutting off, or shortening, is where **truncate** comes from. The source is possibly PIE's *\*tere-*.

## Six Degrees of Separation

Six sets of unlikely etymological bedfellows . . .    . . . and the PIE that binds them:

| | |
|---|---|
| 1. **conjugal** and **joust** | *\*yeng:* to join |
| 2. **cordial** and **courage** | *\*kerd:* heart |
| 3. **granite** and **pomegranate** | *\*gre-no:* grain |
| 4. **ingenious** and **engine** | *\*gene:* to give birth |
| 5. **halogen** and **salami** | *\*sal:* salt |
| 6. **verse** and **versus** | *\*wer:* to turn or bend |

# 3.
# THE EARLIEST ENGLISH WASN'T ENGLISH AT ALL

In Pat Conroy's novel *Beach Music,* Jack McCall, whose true home is South Carolina's Lowcountry, takes a woman he went to high school with on a tour of his adopted home of Rome. On the itinerary is viewing an ancient tablet whose words the emperor Claudius had inscribed after his successful conquest of a smallish island to the west. Jack points to just four letters carved into the tablet: B-R-I-T.

"This is the first mention of Britannia, the isle of England, in all of history. Our mother tongue began at this spot, Southern girl," he announces grandly.

To which his friend replies: "It gives me a headache."

## Stranger in a familiar land

*Aha!* you may be thinking. *So that first language was Latin.*

Actually, no.

In fact, although Latin would eventually have an outsize influence on English, it barely moved the linguistic needle during its first appearance. This was despite the fact that the ancient Romans controlled what they called Britannia for nearly five hundred years.

But B-R-I-T also indicates the people who inhabited the island when the Romans arrived around 43 BCE: the Britons, or Celts. They had been there, in what they called Britain, for several hundred years.

The two languages, Celtic and Latin, coexisted quite amicably. But that was not the case with the next language that entered Britain, when a mashup of Germanic tribes came barreling through. And unlike the Romans, these folks didn't leave. It was they who kick-started this tongue called English. They also did a pretty good job of kicking the Celts, whom they had little use for, to the far edge of England and beyond.

The B-R-I-T had pretty much gone out of Britannia.

The soon-to-be-English called the Celts *wealas:* "foreigners." The term made the Britons strangers in what had been their own land. Even more stinging was the fact that *wealas* became the basis of "Wales," one of three countries the Britons fled to, along with Scotland and Ireland.

Not surprisingly, the people who live in that country have another, Celtic name for it: Cymru. You'll see it today on signage the moment you cross from England into Wales. It is an echo of *cymry,* meaning "fellow countryman," which is a far cry from "foreigner."

## 'Thanks, we brought our own'

Melvyn Bragg, the author of *The Adventure of English*, says that only about two dozen words from Celtic have survived in English. Some linguists would find that number too low; still, it's hardly a mother lode. Many are place-names, more common in England than the US—Dover, Avon, Thames, Penwortham. Trent, the name of one of the longest rivers in England (and also of a few US cities), comes from the Celtic term for "wanderer," and rivers are known to meander.

"How could it be," muses Bragg, "that so few Celtic words infiltrated a language which was to grow by embracing infiltration?"

One reason for the paucity of Celtic words we English speakers carry on our tongues is that the Germanic groups used their own language for writing, leaving Celtic for more colloquial use. This written language is what we know as Old English, which only a few of us can read anymore. Here—have a go:

*e pluribus* **ENGLISH**

> Hwæt. We Gardena in geardagum,
> þeodcyninga, þrym gefrunon,
> hu ða æþelingas ellen fremedon.

If you're thinking that these must be the opening lines of *Beowulf,* believed to have been written down in the eighth century, you are correct. (For the truly intrepid, you can find the epic poem in Old English in its entirety on the Poetry Foundation website.)

There are no comparable early texts in Celtic that we can turn to. Even so, as the linguaphile and cognitive neuroscientist Kieran O'Mahony points out, there are stone pillars dating back to at least the sixth century containing the alphabet called Ogham, a precursor to the Gaelic languages. "Several of them are on our ancestral farm," adds O'Mahony, who, as you no doubt guessed, is Irish.

The author Joy Chant posited another theory for the written silence, in her book *The High Kings.* She maintained that storytelling among the Celts was often considered so sacred that it was forbidden to write down the tales and poems the bards recited.

"Many, probably at one time all, stories were held to have specific powers of blessing and protection; they were in the old and literal sense spells."

## The P's, Q's, and do's of Celtic

Whatever the reasons for the scarcity, Celtic actually did leave a significant stamp on English, even if not a surfeit of words. As the linguist John McWhorter tells us, "Old English ... was a Germanic language that was deeply tinctured by Celtic grammar ... ." One trace of this tincturing is the way English speakers use "do." Rather than "I walk not," in English it's "I do not walk." Says McWhorter: "The only languages in the world that use *do* in the way that English does, and exactly that way, are Celtic ones."

Just imagine what our marriage vows might be without that whisper of Celtic language when we utter the life-changing refrain of "I do."

To say "Celtic language" is oversimplifying its diversity. There are two main families, the P-Celtic and the Q-Celtic. The Q-Celtic languages include Irish, Scottish Gaelic, and Manx. The P-Celtic languages include

Breton, Welsh, and Cornish. It is this last one, Cornish, that proved to be the holdout in the land that became England.

## Camelot endures

While most of the Celts ended up settling outside of England, there remained one stronghold in the far southwest corner of the country: the county of Cornwall. Somewhat astonishingly, given the many different languages that spread through the land, the Celts were able to hold onto their language there—Cornish—for centuries. It took the Prayer Book Rebellion of 1549 to begin its slide. The revolt was an unsuccessful attempt by the Cornish and some others to resist the new Anglican Book of Common Prayer, which was written in English.

(Not too long after, in 1604, King James I of England brought the word "Britain" back in favor, proclaiming himself king of Great Britain, ruler of both Scotland and England. B-R-I-T was back.)

Nevertheless, the Cornwall of Celtic times left us with a story so compelling that it *was* written down, several times, the first being in the twelfth century. Drawing in part from a Welsh legend, an English bishop named Geoffrey of Monmouth wrote his work not in English but in Latin. It was the story of Arthur, son of Uther Pendragon, and his Knights of the Roundtable. Tintagel Castle, on Cornwall's turbulent coast, is said to be King Arthur's birthplace, and the cave beneath it Merlin's lair.

Arthur was intent on defeating the Saxons (read: English). While his legend has endured, some say that Arthur himself lives on in the form of a black, raven-like bird with red beak and claws called the Cornish chough. In August 2021, the BBC reported that a record number of choughs were born in Cornwall. Could it be the sign of a second Arthurian quest?

## Hearing Echoes through Shakespeare's Ears

In their *Shakespeare Miscellany,* the father-and-son coauthors David Crystal and Ben Crystal share with us how actors in some of Shakespeare's plays would maintain Welsh, Irish, and Scottish pronunciations of certain English words. Here are a few of those echoing sounds:

- Where the English pronunciation is "battle," the Welsh is "pattle." The English "valorous" spoken with a Welsh tongue sounds "falorous."
- Both Welsh and Scottish deliver "sall" for the English "shall." The English "both" becomes the Scottish "bath," while "mass" becomes "mess."
- Irish is represented with "be," which in English would be pronounced "by." And Irish "beseeched" while English "besieged." Here we'll slide in this extra from O'Mahony, one of whose six languages is (no surprise) Irish Gaelic. He points out that in Irish, words with more than one syllable emphasize the one that's up first. But there's an exception, as there often is with languages. It's the double ee—the lenition, as he calls it—and when there are double letters, as in "beseeched," that syllable snags the emphasis. So the Irish pronunciation would sound quite familiar to English ears.

## Welsh, Irish, and Scottish Galore

Although few original Celtic words have survived, the later Welsh, Irish, and Scottish languages all have words that English speakers recognize.

But why say "galore" if there aren't bucketfuls of words? For starters, **galore** is one of those drops in the bucket. It comes from the Irish Gaelic *go leor* and the Scottish Gaelic *gu léor*. And while today we associate it with plentiful, originally it meant sufficient.

Here are a few more words galore:

Welsh has given us **corgi,** meaning dwarf dog of the kind that Queen Elizabeth II doted on. **Cardigan** comes from the name of a sixth-century Welsh king named Ceredig. **Coracle** is a small round boat. From Irish comes **slew** (from *sluagh,* a multitude).

Thank Scottish for **glamour,** which started off meaning magic, and not always the Disney kind—more like the occult. Nor was the spelling what it is today. *"And you, deep-read in hell's black grammar, Warlocks and witches,"* scowled Robert Burns in a 1789 poem. That "grammar" would be "glamour": any kind of scholarship, including grammatical, was comparable to casting a spell. Scottish also gave us a word worth fussing about: **kerfuffle** (or in the Scottish, *curfuffle*). Cause a kerfuffle, and someone's feathers you'll ruffle.

## Puzzling over 'Penguin'

Imagine that you're a Church of England cleric who's been assigned as chaplain of a ship that's sailing around the world. It's 1578, so it's going to be a long trip. But it will be an interesting one: you are aboard Sir Francis Drake's *Golden Hind*. This was the tour of duty that Francis Fletcher found himself on, and he kept detailed notes of the voyage, including the days sailing to the tip of South America.

A century later, a document presented as a transcript of these notes includes this entry from Fletcher: "infinite were the number of fowles, which the Welsh men named Penguin."

This is how the editors of the *Oxford English Dictionary* tell the tale, and two other works around Fletcher's era pile on. Even so, more corroboration would be helpful, the *OED* maintains, as it devotes nearly two columns of its hefty print edition to puzzling over **penguin**. Merriam-Webster delivers this more succinct verdict: "perhaps from Welsh *pen gwyn* white head."

## Walking the Talk with *Brogue*

An accent by another name, when Irish and Scots speakers are involved, is a brogue. But those sturdy, sensible shoes that both men and women wear are also brogues, distant echoes of the rough-and-tumble footwear that Highlanders would sport. **Brogue,** in fact, comes from the Irish word for shoe. So how does it also come to mean that distinctive Gaelic accent? From an old and not very flattering way to describe that accent. Robert McCrum, William Cran, and Robert MacNeil, the authors of *The Story of English,* explain: "The Irishman was said to speak with 'a shoe on his tongue.'" We should all speak with such a light, lilting step. "People pay a fortune today to speak with that *bróg,*" points out O'Mahony, who came by his naturally.

## For Crying Out Loud

**Keen** is likely to make you weep when you hear this Irish verb in action. That's just what it means (from *Caoiním,* I wail, with all the vowels delivering the "ee" sound in "keen"). It often signifies a funeral. Just to distress you more, in Irish folklore there's a fairy whose singing prophesizes a death. Her anguished voice is that of a **banshee**: *bean sídhe.*

O'Mahony explains how the sound of "banshee" came about linguistically. The placement of the (silent) h in *sídhe,* he says, "makes the 'd' go silent, and the result is sí. The s is slender because of the i and therefore is pronounced 'sh.' Hence banshee."

Turns out that award-winning movie, *The Banshees of Inisherin,* gives a lot away just in the title.

## An *Eburāka* State of Mind?

The city known as New Amsterdam when the Dutch appropriated it became, of course, New York when the English snatched it. They named it in honor of England's Duke of York.

In his book about New York City place-names, the geographer Joshua Jelly-Schapiro tells us that "York" began its linguistic life as Celtic, where it was *Eburāka*. It means "a place of the yew tree."

Think Billy Joel might consider recording a "New Yew State of Mind"?

## Would You Swallow Such Flummery?

**Flummery** is from the Welsh *llymru*. It started off in the seventeenth century as a rather unappetizing-sounding oatmeal dish. It got better over the years as it got sweeter, and is still found in various iterations among British recipes.

But "flummery" has also come to mean flattery in its most vacuous form. Unless you're in the food section, that's how you'll likely find it used today. The distinction is akin to **trifle** being both an English dessert and something that's of little value.

## Where You Can Find Cornish Consumed in the US

The same word root that gives us *pasta* gives us **pasty**, and the first syllable is pronounced the same way. Cornish pasties are a particular combination of meat and vegetables wrapped in a crescent of dough and baked. The shape made it easy for miners' fingers to grasp as they tucked into their nutritious meal while working Cornwall's tin mines.

If you've seen, and perhaps tasted, something matching this description in the Upper Peninsula of Michigan, it's no coincidence. Cornish miners who immigrated to the US brought their taste for this savory pie with them, when they went to work in Michigan's iron mines.

The UK's Cornish Pasty Association ensures that only those tasty crescents that are made in Cornwall can legitimately be called Cornish pasty. Also: it's only Cornish if the dough is crimped along the edges.

If you'd like to try your hand at making one, here's the recipe for the real deal: https://cornishpastyassociation.co.uk/about-the-pasty/make-your-own-genuine-cornish-pasty. Of course, to make them truly official, you'll want to bake them in Cornwall.

## Manx: The Language with Nine Lives?

The Isle of Man, between England and Ireland, is known for its cat with no tail. Manx cats have a stub where other felines have a swisher. But though they may be unusual, this ancient breed is not in danger of disappearing. You can say the same of another ancient Celtic breed: the Manx language.

Despite UNESCO briefly declaring in 2009 that the language was extinct, it's not. But it came close, which is why there's a move afoot on the island to make the native language as ubiquitous as the native cats. Today you can hear Manx in schools, read it on tombstones, and listen to it sung in pubs—where a Manx speaker might greet you with *Slaynt vie!* (Cheers!)

# 4.
# THE ENGLISH IS COMING! THE ENGLISH IS COMING!

In 1939, a Harvard student who had gone to England was allowed to observe as members of the Houses of Parliament debated. He listened in particular as the First Lord of the Admiralty exhorted the British Government to heed the monstrous threat of Adolf Hitler. The American was struck by how the speaker delivered his remarks—his cadence, his choice of words.

The speaker was Winston Churchill, whose early warnings about the Third Reich proved prescient. Churchill became Britain's prime minister in May 1940, when Britain was well into the Second World War. As the American radio journalist Edward R. Murrow said of him, "He mobilized the English language and sent it into battle." (And a good thing, because Churchill's war of words was at times one of Britain's best weapons.)

Now all of Britain could hear the galvanizing rhetoric of Churchill, and on a regular basis, as BBC Radio broadcasted his messages. Here is an excerpt from one of many that mobilized the English people:

> We shall fight on the beaches, we shall fight on the landing grounds, we shall fight in the fields and in the streets, we shall fight in the hills; we shall never surrender.

In this famous passage, one word differs from all the others, but which? And who was the American who had listened so intently to Churchill?

*To be continued . . .*

―――

## The Four Musketeers, *Englisc* Style

They were known as invaders before they were known as English (*Englisc* is how they referred to themselves). The various Germanic tribes that came clattering into England beginning in the fifth century included the Jutes, the Angles, and the Saxons. Call them the Three Musketeers of Old English.

*Not so fast,* say the Frisians.

Actually, says the linguist John McWhorter. The Frisians were a fourth Germanic tribe that arrived—the D'Artagnan of the lot, and actually more integral to the establishment of Old English than the other three.

Unlike those other three, who arrived from parts of Germany and Denmark, the Frisians came from the Netherlands. And it is Old Frisian that Old English more resembles. Try this Frisian phrase, courtesy of McCrum, Cran, and MacNeil: *in kopke koffe.* It's not that far from its English descendant: "a cup of coffee."

Moreover, McWhorter points out that even in the modern forms of both Dutch and English, they're the only languages with a Germanic lineage that have the vowel sound you hear in, for example, "ran" and "cat."

## Curse and coo—woohoo!

Although it wouldn't come to the fore until after 1066 and the arrival of the Norman French (which coincidentally was when Old English started to fade), this early medieval English laid the groundwork for a dual personality in our language that has endured ever since.

English is a Jekyll and Hyde character. We curse like an Englisc and coo like a Norman. On one side of our mouth we talk brief and brusque (Englisc/Germanic). On the other we talk long and languid (Norman/Romance). Germanics sweat. Normans perspire. Germanics have lamb and deer. French have mutton and venison.

This bifurcation is an oversimplification, of course. But it is true that we tap the Germanic tip of our tongue for the most common words in English, many of which are the shorter words. Then we draw from a considerable cache of Romance words (**cache** being one of them) to add a certain **cachet** (yep, that one, too) to our sentences.

The linguist Anatoly Liberman observes that "numerically, words of Romance origin predominate in the vocabulary of the modern language, even though the most frequent words (*come, go, . . . foot, hand, . . . bread, water*) are usually Germanic." And, Liberman says, "native English words are, as a rule, monosyllabic." In other words: short.

The late John Barton, a cofounder of the Royal Shakespeare Company, points to Shakespeare's genius for juxtaposing the short nouns with "the high phrases," as Barton called them. "The living power of the language," he added, "comes from the interplay of the two." To borrow from the Bard: 'tis true, even today.

## *The Churchill story, continued . . .*

Within that passage of Churchill's, according to McCrum, Cran, and MacNeil, the word that's different is the one that is not Germanic: "surrender." It is the only English among those rousing words that did not hark back to early English.

**Surrender** comes from Norman French, the Norman indicating France's Normandy region. How fitting, because this is where the Allied Forces carried out the D-Day invasion of World War II to ensure that, for the Allies, there would be no surrender.

As for the American who was listening to Churchill: it was John F. Kennedy, who accompanied his father to England during Joseph P. Kennedy's ambassadorship to Britain.

When John Kennedy became president in 1961, his declamations were equal to Churchill's. And he selected his words just as strategically. He often sent into his own battles the short, forthright early-English speech to undergird such lofty, metaphor-rich language as this: "And if a beachhead of cooperation may push back the jungle to suspicion, let both sides join in creating a new endeavor. . . ."

That sentence is from Kennedy's inaugural address. But it is not the sentence that is imprinted into American memory. Although a speaker of Old English might not recognize every word in what became the iconic statement from Kennedy's inaugural address ("country" was not then in the lexicon, only "land"), he or she would be intimately acquainted with most of them:

"Ask not what your country can do for you—ask what you can do for your country."

## Pop Quiz #1: What Classic Twentieth-Century Epic Owes Some of Its Magic to Old English?

Yes, it's *The Lord of the Rings* trilogy. Author J.R.R. Tolkien, an Oxford professor of English literature, was a foremost scholar of Old English. He translated *Beowulf* in 1926, and the Old English epic poem is credited with being an inspiration for Tolkien's own epic.

Try reading this morsel of Tolkien's trilogy in Old English:

Hwær is se hring? (Where is the ring?)
Hwæth ring? (What ring?)

## What Does 'Arcane' Have to Do with Porcelain Teacups... and Old English?

The elite of eighteenth-century Europe were obsessed with porcelain. A Chinese creation that turned items like teacups into delicate vessels that could still withstand the heat of boiled water, porcelain was like nothing the Europeans had ever seen. Just how, they wondered as they sipped their tea from Meissen china cups, did the Chinese render the porcelain so white? (The secret was a white clay called kaolin, the English spelling for the name of the hill in China where the clay was mined.)

The mania for porcelain led to one of those long-g-g-g German words that seem so ironic, given the shortness of so many English words of Germanic origin. The word was Porzellankrankheit, which meant "porcelain sickness." (Yes, it was a thing.)

*Interesting,* you might say, *but how does "arcane" fit into all this?*

Before the Europeans cracked the code on kaolin, they called this mysterious porcelain paste arcanum, a Latin word meaning a hidden thing or mystery. It's where we get **arcane,** indicating something obscure.

*Yeah fine whatever,* you might be saying by now, *but what's that got to do with Old English?*

**Arcane** comes from *arca,* meaning a chest or large box. That Latin word had an Old English equivalent whose spelling wasn't far off: *earc.* We know it as **ark,** the kind we associate with the biblical Noah, who built a very large box indeed.

## Night and Day, or: Those Quirky Compound Words

Despite their frequent brevity, Old English words can be longish, too. This is thanks to the predilection of Englisc speakers for creating compound words, something we speakers of Modern English share a penchant for—witness: website, login, upload.

Kevin Stroud, in his *History of English* podcast, and Hana Videen, in her Old English *Wordhord* blog (*wordhord* coming from the Old English for a collection of words), are among those who regale us with these compound creations.

**Fortnight,** for example, comes from the Old English for "fourteen night." British English uses it often as shorthand for two weeks; American English, not so much. But how to count the days in Old English? With "day's eye," a compound derived from a certain flower whose petals unfurl with the dawn and fold at dusk: the **daisy.**

Some of these compound words are known as kennings. These are metaphors used for poetic effect; *Beowulf* abounds with them. Many of them may now seem to be beyond our **ken** (to summon the well-worn phrase that uses the root of kenning, which is ken: to cause to know). But before you look at the answers, see what you can make of these delightful head-scratchers:

| | | |
|---|---|---|
| bone-house | morgenmete | swan's road |
| hoard-locker | sea wood | war-guard |
| life-wound | sin-forced | whale-road |
| malicework | sky-candle | |

**Answers:**
1. bone-house . . . . . . . . . . . . . . . . . body
2. hoard-locker . . . . . . . . . . . the mind
3. life-wound . . . . . . . . . mortal wound
4. malicework . . . . . . . . . . destruction
5. morgenmete . . . . . . . . . . . breakfast
6. sea wood . . . . . . . . . . . . . . . . . . . ship
7. sin-forced . . . . . . . . . . . . . . . . . . feud
8. sky-candle . . . . . . . . . . . . . . . . . . sun
9. swan's road . . . . . . . . . . . . . . . ocean
10. war-guard . . . . . . . . . . . . . . . . . king
11. whale-road . . . . . . . . . . . . . . . . . sea

## Pop Quiz #2: What's the Old English Word That's Both a Greeting and a Grog?

*Westu Théoden hal,* as Tolkien presented the greeting. Don't recognize it? Try it in grog form: **wassail.** The salutation translates as a wish of good health to you; with a cup of wassail in hand, you can drink to it.

## That Wulf at the Door Is Your Husband

Thank Old English for **werewolf** (originally *werewulf*), a man who can morph into a wolf. We should probably thank the Dutch *weerwolf* and the German *werwolf* while we're at it. *Werewulf* also shares the same piece of PIE, *\*wi-ro*, as the Latin-based *virile*. *Wer* could also indicate that wolf man was married, a rather unsettling thought. But "husband" eventually pushed him out.

# 5.
# BLESS THOSE ROMANS, THEY FINALLY GOT RELIGION

The Roman Empire might have called it quits in Britain in the fifth century CE, but in a way it was just the end of one kind of rule and the beginning of another: the Christian religion.

The late sixth century is when Pope Gregory of Rome dispatched a monk named Augustine to Britain. His mission was to convert the masses to Catholicism (which is what this early Christianity was). The man who would become the first Archbishop of Canterbury, and eventually St. Augustine, didn't have to start from scratch.

Not all the Romans had left Britain earlier, and some were already Christians. In fact, as early as the fourth century, the Roman Emperor Constantine (he of Constantinople fame) was championing the religion. Among Britain's "Romano-British Christian" families, as the British Library describes them, was one with a son named Maewyn Succat. If the name doesn't sound familiar, it's because we know him as St. Patrick. He was captured by Irish warriors as a teenager and taken from Britain to Ireland.

With a new faith came a host of new words. They were mainly from Latin, but with some Greek as well. For many the new faith signaled good news, and the Greek-to-Latin *evangelium* came to mean this.

While it's easy to see how this became our **evangelical**, it also set the stage for *godspel,* or as we know it now, **gospel.**

## The key to Greek

The Greek influence was due, in part, to the fact that the Catholic Mass was also celebrated in Greek. Prior to the fourth century, according to the Vatican, "here and there the readings [contained in the Mass] were customarily read in Greek, and afterwards translated into Latin; thus an almost bi-lingual Mass existed." The reason, the Vatican says, "seems simply to have originated from the need to promote participation among those faithful who could not yet understand Latin."

Thank Greek for **angel** (from the Greek for messenger) and **psalm,** which originally alluded to playing a stringed instrument such as a harp. **Baptism** meant to immerse in water, and pretty much still does. The source of a word like **hosanna**, which English speakers know to mean an exclamation of praise, goes back even earlier than the Greek, to the Hebrew, where it was a cry for deliverance: "pray, save us!"

Latin and English would absorb these words over time. Rome, as we know, wasn't built in a day, nor English in a lifetime.

## Some immortal Latin

**Salvation** comes from the Latin *salvare,* or save (as with a soul). **Sacred** and **consecrate** both come from *sacrare.* Not all the words suggest such veneration, though: **infidel** is one who is not a believer, although the word has just the opposite embedded in it: *fidelis,* or, in the ecclesiastical sense, **faithful.** And thus the Christmas carol "O Come, All Ye Faithful," when sung in Latin, begins with *Adeste, Fidelis.*

Then there's the surprise of **pagan.** Yes, it's from Latin, *paganus*; and yes, it did eventually come to refer to someone who did not practice the Christian, Jewish, or Islamic faith. But that isn't how it started out.

The original meaning of *paganus* is one who lived in the country. Among the Roman military, it was also someone who was a civilian. As far as Roman soldiers were concerned, being a civilian was tantamount to being incompetent. Interestingly, Christianity turned that idea on its head and adopted the concept of "soldiers of Christ."

**Imprimatur**, from the Latin *imprimere*, in its literal sense means to print, although it came to mean permission to print. Certain books dealing with the Catholic faith will contain the word *imprimatur*, indicating that the book's content aligns with the Church's teaching. But today, "imprimatur" can indicate any kind of approval. It's a religious term that's gone secular, and it's not the only one.

## Some Curious Couples That Christianity Begat

**Vulgate and vulgar.** In order to make the Bible more accessible to the masses, in the fourth century the scholar St. Jerome translated versions in earlier languages—Aramaic, Hebrew, Greek, Latin—into a more accessible Latin version. This new Latin Vulgate caught on instantly with the common folk, or *vulgus*, and was an enduring success. As Victoria M. Tufano, director of liturgy at Ascension Catholic Church in Oak Park, Illinois, points out, "The instinct of Christianity has always been that people should worship in a language they understand."

In English, *vulgus* eventually evolved into "vulgar," meaning not just common but coarse. This meaning, too, has endured.

**Pope and poplin.** For centuries the Church's *papa*, or pope, has worn vestments of rich fabric. One such was a silk and wool fabric made in Avignon, France, that the French created in the fifteenth century. They named it *papeline* to honor the pope, whose residence was then in Avignon. From this came "poplin."

**Bull and bill.** This is the papal bull we're talking about. It's a stumper of a way to describe a papal edict until we learn that this bull is from the Latin *bulla*, for a document that has been sealed. And a bill, as in a congressional bill, is a similar kind of decree, the word evolving from the same *bulla*. Ditto for "bulletin."

But *bulla* meant more than just the document; it was what authenticated it as well. *Bulla* also indicated a round protuberance. This would have been a reference to the actual seal that signaled the official status of the papal bull. It is said to have taken the shape of an amulet worn around the neck.

**Propaganda and propaganda.** Yes, it's the same word twice. As Ben Zimmer, formerly the "Word on the Street" columnist for *The Wall Street Journal*, tells us, the first *propaganda* refers to one of those papal bulls. Issued in 1622, it called for the *Congregatio de Propaganda Fide*, which you've probably guessed meant Congregation for the Propagation of the Faith. This *propaganda* simply meant "a spreading"; no pejorative connotation attached.

That more negative definition started to take hold in the late 1700s, when the word took on a secular use as a description of political doctrines. The Soviet Union gave it a Russian spritz in the 1920s, combining its two long words for "agitation" and "propaganda" into the single, and somewhat sinister, "agitprop."

**Conclave and conclave.** Another same-word-twice example, and once again with the word spelled the same in both English and Latin. A conclave started off as a room with a lock (and therefore a key—*clavis*). This made it an ideal place for cardinals to convene when they were holding their top-secret election of a new pope. The English conclave shed the papal reference and now means the gathering—secret or otherwise—of a group with a common interest.

## A Mass with a Mission

The culmination of the liturgical service called the Mass is the celebration of the Eucharist, commonly known as taking Communion. (**Eucharist**, btw, comes not from Latin but from the Greek *eukharistia*, meaning "thanksgiving.") The Mass concludes shortly after Communion with the priest bidding congregants to go in peace.

Until fairly recently, the wording of this dismissal was "The Mass is ended, go in peace." It hewed closely to the original Latin of *Ite, missa est,* which meant "Go, it is sent." From *missa* (*mittere:* to send) came the word Mass—and also the word **mission.**

## A Rose Is a Rose Is a Rosary

The circular string of beads that many Catholics use to count off certain prayers is called a **rosary.** While prayer beads are found in numerous religions, it's primarily Catholics who register the word rosary. Its root stems from a well-known flower—yes, you guessed it: the rose. (President Reagan, by the way, declared the rose the national flower of the United States.)

The pre-Christian Romans knew all about roses: they were the flower of the sensual goddess Venus. The early Christian Romans thought that made the rose a bit racy: too pagan a symbol, according to Simon Morley, the author of *By Any Other Name.*

Over time, though, this previously sniffed-at pagan symbol would, like others, be pressed into service for a Christian one. In fact, so sacred a figure would the rose become that it blossomed into a symbol of the Virgin Mary, the mother of Jesus Christ.

Thus the centuries-old German Christmas carol known in English as "Lo, how a rose e'er blooming" is a song of Mary, giving birth to her only son. (Hear it on YouTube, among other sites: https://www.youtube.com/watch?v=J4-bQJ64sho.)

As for the rosary? The Latin it derives from, *rosarium,* means "rose garden."

## *Sanctus* and the Sacred Space of Forty Days

From the Latin *sanctus,* or holy, comes **sanctuary.** For more than three hundred years in England, a Christian church was considered a sanctuary. If you were a fugitive running from the law during those years, you were in luck: when you entered a Christian church—large or small, didn't matter—you were safe from your pursuers. The right of sanctuary protected you; it was, to use another offspring of *sanctus*, **sacrosanct.**

Much the same was true in France. It's what led the fictitious Quasimodo of Victor Hugo's *Hunchback of Notre Dame* novel to thrice cry "Sanctuary!" as he rescued the woman he loved who had been framed for a murder. While most such flights to sanctuary probably weren't as cinematic, there were highly ritualistic elements to them.

In northern England, for example, the small town of Beverley is completely and happily consumed by its massive minster (which is a bit like saying "wet water," as minster denotes large). Of the four main roads that led to Beverley in medieval times, each bore a stone cross. Venture beyond any one of them, and even though the minster was still about two miles away, you were safe. These were sanctuary stones, and they marked the beginning of a kind of religious DMZ.

Not all churches had sanctuary stones, but most had a metal ring affixed to their front door—the sanctuary knocker. A knock and the declaration of "I claim sanctuary" gained you entrance and a safe haven, if only for a specified time: usually forty days.

The number forty is found throughout scripture. Moses was on Mount Sinai for forty days and nights. After fleeing from the Egyptians, the Israelites spent forty years in the desert. Christ fasted forty days and nights before beginning his divine work; this set the time frame for the Lenten observance by many Christians. (Don't count the Sundays.)

Sometimes the circumstances you were fleeing from resolved themselves during those forty days, especially if repentance was involved. Other times, if you wanted to remain free after the forty, you had to leave the country, and fast.

English sanctuary laws were in effect from 1300 to 1624. But although it was Christianity that made them possible, the idea of providing asylum was actually a pre-Christian one, found among polytheist—aka pagan— religions.

## Paganus Redux

Those pagans again—a Christian England just couldn't get away from them. But if *paganus* started off meaning something close to country bumpkin, it took on a more repellent trapping in England by June 8, 793. A letter by a scholar of the time decried the horror of that day:

> Never before has such terror appeared in Britain as we have now suffered from a pagan race.

The Vikings had landed at Lindisfarne in northeast England, and all unholy hell had broken loose. Talk about *paganus*. This lot wasn't just from the country; it seemed like they were from the back of beyond.

# 6.
## COMES A NORSEMAN: VIKINGS TAKE LOOT, LEAVE LANGUAGE

Lindisfarne, a small island off the far northeast coast of England, housed a wealthy monastery that the Vikings promptly sacked. But it was not, as is sometimes believed, the Vikings' first such raiding rodeo in Britain. As the bioarcheologist and Viking expert Cat Jarman reminds us in her book, *River Kings*, there had been at least one raid elsewhere six years earlier.

Regardless, Lindisfarne grabbed the historical headlines. The monastery was renowned for its Lindisfarne Gospels, a sumptuous illuminated manuscript that the British Library says "has long been acclaimed as the most spectacular manuscript to survive from Anglo-Saxon England." When the Vikings sailed from what today we call Scandinavia to pay their infamous visit on 8 June 793, they left the manuscript pages alone. After all, those gospels were written in Latin and Old English, nothing like the runic language these Norsemen wrote with.

The Vikings' preference for "exotic looted objects," as Jarman describes it, ran more to items like "fragments of stunning clip-carved book covers [that they] repurposed into brooches or a near-perfect reliquary shrine." That shrine, most especially, for its gold and silver.

## Rhymes with 'raid'

While these future Swedes, Danes, and Norwegians were indeed ruthless raiders ("brutally enterprising," as one contemporary Brit who can claim Danish heritage describes them), they were also sophisticated traders. They traveled west, as to England and later North America; east, into Ukraine and beyond; and also south to France, Spain, and Morocco. England was just one of many stops, but it was not merely a smash-and-grab gig. It was more like: raid-leads-to-trade-leads-to-stayed. (And bathed, which they did more frequently than those Englisc did—thus our **bask**, which some language sleuths believe evolved from Old Norse *bathe*.)

The Vikings first set up temporary encampments in England but eventually set down permanent roots. In fact, so many of the Danes settled in northeastern England that for a time it was called Danelaw. "By the end of the Viking Age, in the mid-eleventh century," writes Jarman, "the Scandinavians' impact on Britain would be profound, affecting everything from the development of towns to the currency, culture, language and art."

## It left the Vikings speechless

Not that all this happened without some serious hiccups. When in the ninth century the Vikings tried to overrun the entirety of England, in particular the prized southwest kingdom of Wessex, they ran up against the fierce resistance of Alfred, Wessex's king. Alfred prevailed: he not only kept his existing kingdom through battle and treaty, but then expanded it through (drum roll here) language.

"Alfred quite consciously used the English language as a means of creating a sense of national identity," observe McCrum, Cran, and MacNeil in *The Story of English*. His stroke of genius, say the authors, "was his inspiration to use English, not Latin, as the basis for the education of his people."

But first, Alfred had to learn the Latin himself.

Which he did, in his late thirties, so he could translate important Latin writings into English. Being biliterate helped him take his place in history as Alfred the Great.

## Short & bleak

Even so, when it came to linguistic invasions into the English language, Vikings could give as good as they got as far as short, punchy words. (Guess where **give** and **get** come from?) McCrum, Cran, and MacNeil estimate that around nine hundred words that made their way from the Norse languages into English were "typically plain-syllabled."

And some were downright gloomy, as Kevin Stroud, the host of *The History of English* podcast, has observed. "Very often—not always—but very often, they have a negative connotation," he says.

How do **dank**, **dreg**, **grime**, **muck**, and **scab** strike you? These are some—but not all—of Stroud's gloomy examples. A couple more: "English gives us right, and actually also gives us the word straight, but Old Norse gives us **wrong** and **crooked**."

And yet, the real kicker lay not with the glum but with the grammar. By introducing three short words we use all day long, the Vikings left an indelible mark on the language.

## Triple threat

They, them, their.

And there you have them. Now English had this handy set of third-person plural pronouns that had it all over the Old English version.

"Pronouns do not change very often in the history of a language," observes David Crystal, "and to see one set of forms replaced by another is truly noteworthy."

Okay, maybe you had to be there, but this is what happens when you not only raid and trade but then stay. As the Vikings settled in, they succeeded in settling down the language... somewhat. By simplifying some of the grammatical structure of English, it meant that the natives and the Norse could better understand one another.

So while it's true that the French made a huge impact on English with the number of words they added, the Vikings may have one-upped them with their sentence structure and stolen their linguistic thunder. (Note the three pronouns in that sentence.)

But guess where those *Normandy* French originated? (Hint: *Norman*, as in Norseman.)

As for those so-called *paganus* that first barged into England in the eighth century, it wasn't all that long before the Vikings took something else of the country's: its Christian religion. As Gareth Williams, a curator at the British Museum, points out, "the Vikings had many gods, and it was no problem for them to accept the Christian god alongside their own."

## What Do These Seven Words Have in Common?

scant
scare
scorch
scrub
skill
skillet
sky

Yes! They're all from the Vikings. Extra credit if you noticed that they all possess the "sk" sound, which many Viking-to-English words do. The Viking "sky," by the way, meant the English "cloud."

## No Thrill in This Thrall

In English we might say that someone **enthralled** us—meaning left us spellbound. It's a good feeling. Now let's walk back that word to "thrall." It holds a stronger suggestion of captivity—we are "in thrall to" someone or something. Not always a good feeling. Go back even further, to the word's root: the Old Norse word *throell,* meaning the worst kind of captivity: slavery. Those who were enslaved were referred to as *trell*.

## Let Them Eat Skate

**Skate**, as in the type of fish, is courtesy of the Vikings. But you could just as easily have titled this little section "Let them eat cake," and you'd still be in Viking World.

**Cake** was another one of their words, along with an ingredient in many cakes: **egg.** The Vikings also used the word in the expression "egg on," which they were no doubt good at doing.

## So Like What We Think Would Be a Viking

Old stereotypes die hard, and some don't die at all. So it often is with the Vikings. (**Die**, btw, can be traced to Old Norse.) It may come as little surprise, then, that these words were Old Norse before they were English.

**Berserk.** Back in the day, "berserk" indicated a fearful warrior—a Viking, in other words. The word may have evolved from "bare shirt," as this was part of the warrior (un)dress.

**Ransack.** From the Viking words for "house" and sack."

**Slaughter.** As in butchering meat.

**Outlaw.** Ironically, the Danelaw also gave us "law."

**Take.** But remember the Vikings also gave us **give**—and **gift**, in the sense of talent. And so we land on this next little list:

## So Not Like What We Think Would Be a Viking

Here are some words the Vikings gave English that poke holes in the stereotype.

**Freckle.** Take it back to PIE and you find "scatter," a perfect segue into "freckle."

**Gasp.** The Old Norse word for opening the mouth wide was *gaph*, something we tend to do when we gasp.

**Sleuth.** This started off in Old Norse as meaning the track of an animal or person. In English, "sleuth" started off as "sleuthhound," which suggests some creature following that track.

*e pluribus* **ENGLISH**

# Great Scot—They're Not!

Who would have guessed that these two words were Old Norse rather than Celtic? Just when you think you've mastered two more pieces of this jigsaw puzzle called English . . . you haven't. English can be so maddeningly wonderful.

**scot.** *Oh come on, seriously?* you may be thinking. Seriously, when the s is lowercase, "scot" has nothing to do with Scotland or the Scots. This scot is Old Norse for "contribution." The expression we still use today of "getting off scot-free" means someone not having to pay, often metaphorically speaking.

**kilt.** The Scots may wear them but it's the Vikings who named them. "Kilt" is Old Norse for the fold of a gathered skirt.

# 7.
# WHAT THE ENGLISC CALLED ARABISC

Even though the Vikings were sophisticated traders in Istanbul and beyond, among some Arabs they were called *al-Madjus*, or fire worshippers. At the time, it was another way to say heathen. (Once a *paganus* . . . )

That's not an Arabic term that made it into English. But a number of others did. Given the wanton word sponge that English is, this should come as no surprise. But two aspects of the Arabic loanwords stand out.

## Not all in the family

The first is that Arabic is a Semitic language, like Aramaic and Hebrew. That's a different language family from the Indo-European gang that English is part of. While hardly the stuff of Montague and Capulet drama, it speaks to how languages follow their own paths, rather like willful teenagers, heedless of whatever family we say they belong to.

The second is that the Arabic loanwords in English are not the result of a physical invasion of England. Unlike those Frisians, Angles, Saxons, Jutes, Romans, and Norsemen, who would have gone to some trouble to cross that channel and announce themselves, native Arabic speakers never had to show up.

But Arabic-speaking people checked in nearly everywhere else. They were frequent travelers along the Silk Roads, where you were apt to bump into just about anyone—even a Viking. And from the seventh century onward, they were spreading the Islamic religion. As UNESCO observes of the language, "Arabic spread, along with Islam, to far corners of the earth." Asia, northern Africa, western Europe—Muslims covered much of the most traveled parts of the world in their day, bringing with them the language of the divine revelations that the prophet Muhammad received.

## Both direct and indirect routes—and roots—for English

The Arab Academy puts the number of Arabic-derived English words at north of one hundred—for the most part, the result "of years of international trade, conquests, exploration and migration." English lifted some of those words directly from the Arabic playbook, but not all, according to the academy: "others have been indirectly passed down from Arabic through other, older European languages such as Latin, Turkish or French." English's **saffron** and **mattress**, for example, both of Arabic origin, came to English through French when it was an international language of trade.

The Arabs themselves were borrowers as well as word lenders, plucking words from advanced cultures of the time, notably the Persians and the Greeks. Many of the ancient Roman and Greek texts survived thanks to the translations of Arab scholars. By the eighth century, Arabic was also the language of science.

## The language of the Moors: from Africa to Iberia to America

That same century, the Arabic language began an even grander world tour. It started when the Muslims from northern Africa—the Moors—took control of parts of the Iberian Peninsula. They stayed in what is now Portugal for five centuries, and even longer in parts of today's Spain:

until 1492, to be exact (a busy year for Spanish geopolitical interests). As the scholar and journalist Tunku Varadarajan points out, this would be the only part of western Europe to be conquered by someone other than Europeans.

And it's why, just like the Spanish *ojalá,* the Portuguese equivalent of *oxalá* has Arabic to thank. Arabic influenced both languages, Spanish in particular. In fact, says Gerald Erichsen of ThoughtCo., "the Latin dialect that eventually became Spanish was highly influenced by the invasion of the Arabic-speaking Moors in 711. For many centuries, Latin/Spanish and Arabic existed side by side." (Fittingly, the word **Moors** derives from the Latin *Maurus,* a name for the Islamic Amazigh people living in northern Africa, which in Roman times was called Mauretania.) By the time the Spanish expelled the Moors in the fifteenth century, Erichsen says, "literally thousands of Arabic words had become part of Spanish." Estimates go as high as four thousand words, most of them nouns.

Chalk up the fact that more words influenced Spanish than influenced English to Arabic speakers settling in Spain, where they stayed long enough to even influence place-names. *Guadalajara* is from the Arabic for "valley of stones"; *La Mancha,* from the Arabic for "no water"; and *Alhambra* from the Arabic for "red fort" or "castle."

Like cream poured into coffee, a rich flow of Arabic swirled into the Latin-based language that became Spanish, and those native speakers were soon sailing west across an ocean to land a hemisphere away.

## Do You Recognize These Three Four-Legged Friends?

*Zarafa, ghazal, yarbu:* these Arabic words are, rather surprisingly, the roots for the English names of three animals. In English, all of them begin with "g" (so much for "camel"). The first is probably the easiest to recognize: *zarafa* is **giraffe**. The second is fairly easy: *ghazal* mutates into **gazelle**. That leaves *yarbu,* which is a bit of a leap, on very small feet, to **gerbil**.

# *Al* in the Arabic Family

Much as the Norse language had a preponderance of "sk" words, Arabic has many words with "al." Unlike the Norse, however, "al" indicates a word: "the." Three English words derived from Arabic that begin with this "the" are **algebra** (*álgebra*), **alkali** (*álcali*), and **alfalfa** (*al-faṣfaṣa*).

The Spanish words that brought them to English from the Arabic are *el algebra, el álcali,* and *la alfalfa*. Like other Romance languages, Spanish prefaces nouns with either a masculine or feminine article—either the masculine *el* or feminine *la*—giving these and other Spanish words from Arabic a double dose of "the."

## What the heck happened to the 'the'?

Why didn't English also add the "the"? Because modern English doesn't assign genders to nouns. English does not, for example, have masculine dresses *(los vestidos)* or feminine neckties *(las corbatas)*, as Spanish does. (Other languages, including Romanian and German, have a third, neuter category.)

And yet, so many of the languages that influenced English carry these gender-specific cues for nouns. In French, for example, another heavy-duty influencer, they are *le* and *la*. What gives with English?

First off, it's good to remember that there really is a logic to all that gender assignment in other languages, even though it may not look or sound that way to native-English speakers. It's all connected with what linguists like Anne Curzan, the author of *Gender Shifts in the History of English,* call a "grammatical gender system." (English gets its own back on that logic bit with spelling that frequently defies logic. Find more on that in chapter 10, "Why Can't the English Teach Their Children How to Spell?")

Secondly, as Professor Curzan reminds us, it's *modern* English that doesn't use these genders. Old English, which was around till 1100 or 1150 CE, did have them—all three, in fact: masculine, feminine, neuter. So what happened?

Remember those Vikings, who were settling into England with their Germanic language that was somewhat similar to the English of the time. It's feasible that both language speakers decided to toss those gendered nouns to make it easier to understand each other. There was enough to deal with without tripping over tautologies.

Not such the *paganus* after all.

## Sweet Spot

**Syrup, sherbet, sherbert:** besides a certain sibilance, all three are derived from the Arabic "drink" in its noun and verb form. If you're casting a suspicious eye on "sherbert," it's because you've spotted a spelling variant of "sherbet" that isn't much used these days. It was far more common when sherbert/sherbet entered the English language from its exotic source and its spelling was not yet codified.

Another exoticism that Arabic brought to many tongues (and sweet teeth) is what in English we call **sugar.** The Arabic *sukkar* echoes in the Spanish *azucar,* the German *Zucker,* the Italian *zucchero,* and even the Russian *sakhar*—among others. Can you guess what the Arabic *qandi* is? Right: **candy.**

## The Arabic Word That Americans Almost Sank

You're probably familiar with the word "emir," which started as the Arabic *amir,* or military commander. *Amir* is at the root of the English **admiral.** We automatically associate the word with a naval rank, but its connection to the sea wasn't assured until about the twelfth century, thanks to the seafaring Sicilians.

After that, it seemed that every country with a naval presence boasted of admirals in their tongue's translation of the word. Everyone, that is, except the Americans.

"Our Navy did not have any Admirals until 1862 because many people felt the title too reminiscent of royalty to be used in the republic's navy," explains the Naval History and Heritage Command site. That thinking changed during the American Civil War, when the Navy decided that the high ranking the title conferred was necessary for leadership. The first American naval officer to hold the title was David Farragut, a Virginian who fought on the side of the Union.

## Quick! In Two Seconds: What Year Is This? MDCCCXCVIII

If you figured this out in the allotted time, you are a Latin *wunderkind*. Not that you'd be the first.

The historian Matthew Green tells us that an early-twentieth-century Australian professor named Vere Gordon Childe entertained his dinner guests by doing long division in Roman numerals. He also spoke XVII languages.

Even for those who are familiar with the Latin numbering system, it can take several seconds to string this together: M=1,000; D=500; C=100 x 3; XC=10 subtracted from 100; V=5; III=1 x 3, for one thousand, eight hundred ninety-eight.

Or, more simply: 1898.

And now we know why the Arabic numbering system—actually, Hindu-Arabic—caught on so readily among the Europeans. One delighted fifteenth-century author made it a point to refer to them as "arithmetical numbers," to distinguish them from those clunky Roman numerals.

Plus, the Romans were missing a numeric value that the Arabs deployed: the value of nothing, or as we know it numerically, 0. And the rest, as they say, is 1, 2, 3, 4, 5, 6, 7, 8, 9.

## Who's Morris?

The Morris dancers, who can trace their English folk dancing to the fifteenth century, often celebrate the legend of that very English Robin Hood. But nobody named Morris invented the dance or ever danced it. Rather, the *moreys* dance, as it was originally called, has its root in "Moorish."

## A Match Made in Arabic

All of these English words have their origins in Arabic. See how many original meanings you can match up with the words. *Tip:* one of these words is already correctly matched.

1. alcohol — warehouse
2. algebra — to sift
3. arsenal — appropriate season
4. average — bone setting
5. coffee — house of manufacture
6. garble — eye makeup
7. magazine — damaged goods
8. mocha — Mocha
9. monsoon — notification
10. tariff — wine

Here are the correct matchups:

**1. alcohol: eye makeup**
Okay, a tiny bit of a stretch, but the English word comes from the Arabic *al kohl* (and we all now know what *al* means, right?). *Kohl*, a word for "paint" or "stain," is a fine powder that sometimes encircles the eyes

(it's still popular with some Middle Easterners). Paracelsus, a sixteenth-century Swiss alchemist, advanced the meaning to include a volatile liquid. He was referring to chemical volatility, but you might argue that the intoxicating liquid we now refer to as alcohol can result in those who imbibe becoming just as unstable.

### 2. algebra: bone setting
Actually, "bone setting" was a meaning that English speakers ascribed to *algebra* in the fifteenth century. That's how they may have understood what Arabic-speaking medical workers in Spain were saying. They were close.

*Al jabr* (or *al jebr*) indicated a "reunion of broken parts," according to the *Online Etymology Dictionary*. More broadly, it meant "the reunification." And so, write the math lovers on the Story of Mathematics site, "we can say algebra helps us to reunite bits of information."

### 3. arsenal: house of manufacture
The Arabic *dar as-sina'ah* gave English its arsenal. *Dar* indicates a house, with the second word indicating a person whom today we would call a maker.

The Venetians found the word a handy way to describe a wharf. "As in the Arsenal of the Venetians" is a line that appears in the epic Italian poem *The Divine Comedy* by Dante Alighieri (1265–1321). Ralph Waldo Emerson provided this translation, in 1867.

### 4. average: damaged goods
When goods on a ship were damaged or lost to the sea, insurers covered the loss according to their proportionate value, or average. But take the Arabic connection with a small grain of sea salt. Here's why: "The origin of the word is nautical and from the Mediterranean, which makes Arabic origin possible, but its etymology is still unsolved, though few words have received more etymological investigation," according to the British etymologist Ernest Weekley, in 1921. Some current sources still quote Weekley, and the *Oxford English Dictionary* also weighs in with the same sentiment.

And all these years, we've thought there was nothing special about average.

### 5. coffee: wine

Imagine building a coffeehouse and nobody came. There was a time when Europeans thought little of this Arabic drink called *qahwah*, and their calling it a wine was no compliment. They meant it as "wine of the infidels," a kind of code indicating the non-Christian Arab world. And yet, by the mid-1600s, Europeans had been converted: London alone had in excess of three hundred coffeehouses.

### 6. garble: to sift

Most Mediterranean traders of medieval times would know their language's version of the Arabic *gharbal* (trade and tongues at work once again). They would need to sift through the chaff, or impurities, contained in shipments of spices and other goods. The English version of the word, "garble," latched onto this impurity angle, assigning it to muddled speech that could do with some sifting of the chaff.

### 7. magazine: warehouse

*Makhzan,* or magazine (*khazana* is Arabic for "to store up"), morphed in meaning from general storehouse to ammunition storehouse to the cartridge holder in guns. And then, in a head-scratching leap, to a printed and bound "storehouse" of general-interest writing.

Why the bounce from a literal storehouse to a figurative one? There actually was a connection, according to the *Online Etymology Dictionary*. The first collection of writing to carry the term "magazine" was the eighteenth-century *Gentleman's Magazine*, which borrowed the word from its earlier sense of "printed lists of military stores and information."

### 8. mocha: Mocha

You got this one, right? Mocha, or *al-Mukha*, is a city in Yemen, where these coffee beans are grown and are a centuries-old export.

### 9. monsoon: appropriate season

In Arabic, such an appropriate season, or *mawsim*, could indicate any signal event, such as a pilgrimage or journey. But when Portuguese sailors latched onto the term (*monção* in their language), it started its journey to mean the season when the winds were right for sailing. Now it suggests the torrential rains that accompany them.

**10. tariff: notification**
The Arabic *ta'rif* originally meant any kind of "making known." But as trade in Italy, Sicily, and elsewhere in the Mediterranean expanded, the meaning of the word contracted to indicate a list of products and prices. Once again, it's safe to say that tongues followed trade as far as what certain words came to mean.

# 8.
# IT'S GREEK TO ... WELL, JUST ABOUT EVERYBODY

In an article in *The New York Times* describing an excavation of a new Mayan pyramid in Mexico, the reporter brought home why the find was so significant: "The Maya, with their staggeringly precise calendars, sophisticated hieroglyphs, highly productive agricultural system and ability to predict celestial phenomena such as eclipses, were arguably the most enlightened culture of the New World."

An archeologist quoted in the piece pithily went one better: "'The Maya were truly the Greeks of the ancient Americas.'"

Such stature these Greeks have enjoyed—and by extension, their language.

And yet.

As Albert Baugh and Thomas Cable note in *A History of the English Language*, Greek "does not serve as a language of wider communication." Consider that Greek is spoken by a mere 12.6 million people, 11 million of them in Greece. By comparison, English has somewhere between 350 and 400 million native speakers. The numbers, as so many do, vary by who's reporting them, but the contrast is unmistakable. If English seems too big to fail, Greek seems too small to sail.

And consider: The Greek alphabet directly inspired the one that English uses—but after *alpha, beta, delta,* and *omega,* many of us can reel off the rest of its twenty-four letters only with the help of Google. Fraternity and sorority members, most of whom have adopted Greek letters for their names (hence "the Greek life"), will fare somewhat better. Within the Indo-European family of languages, Greek is basically an aberration, the only kid on the Hellenic block, while all the other family members have plenty of company. (**Hellenic** is essentially a fancier way of saying "Greek.")

And yet.

For many of us, Greek continues to command something approaching reverence when we speak of it . . . even if we don't speak it.

"Greek is a tradition that has institutionally been identified in the West as a source of truth and human knowledge, the origin and paradigm of Western thought and civilization," observes Angeliki Spiropoulou, a scholar at the University of the Peloponnese in Greece.

Westerners are not alone.

Ancient Arab scholars translated the postulates of geometry from a Greek math whiz named Euclid. That translation was then translated into Latin, for the benefit of a wider audience.

This kind of linguistic gymnastics proves a different kind of theorem: namely, that a language need not cover a large swath of the planet to have an outsize influence, as Greek has had on Western thought. It's an argument—in case anyone thinks they need one—for learning a language you love, even if not a lot of the world speaks it.

Just ask Mary Norris, who became enamored with the Greek language while she was a copy editor at *The New Yorker,* to the point of becoming immersed in it. She begins her book, *Greek to Me,* recounting her odyssey (thank you, Homer, whoever you were) with this sweet swoon: "Sing in me, O Muse, of all things Greek that excite the imagination and delight the senses and magnify the lives of mortals . . . you know, the eternal. If that's not too much to ask, Muse." Norris, not surprisingly, has no trouble at all peeling off those twenty-four Greek letters.

## Going one better

Lots of languages have provided English with words for stuff. Greek does, too, but it goes one better: it provides us with the stuff of ideas.

As with the Meditations of Marcus Aurelius, in which the Roman emperor espouses—in Greek—the ideals of the Greek Stoics. In this Meditation, "Either it is a well arranged universe or a **chaos** huddled together, but still a universe," the English translation essentially keeps one of the Greek words, substituting only a "c" for the Greek "k" in *khaos,* meaning abyss. (Ditto **cosmos** and *kosmos*, with its opposite suggestion of harmonious.). Then there are these: Achilles' heel. Platonic idealism. Socratic method. Herculean effort. Hippocratic oath. Pythagorean theorem. Oh, and did we mention: **democracy**.

"The Greeks give us the tools for the work of the mind," says the public philosopher Tom Morris. He learned Greek in college and draws on Greek thought in many of his books, such as *If Aristotle Ran General Motors* and *Plato's Lemonade Stand*. In *The Stoic Art of Living*, he distills the ideas of the Roman Stoics, drawing from their Greek forebears, into practical wisdom for today. "The Greek language, like its culture," Morris says, "is amazing in its clarity and precision."

## Putting it in writing

Let's start with that **alphabet**. The word, conveniently enough, comes from the Greek *alpha* plus *beta*, the names of the first two letters of the Greek alphabet.

The Greeks based their alphabet on the Phoenicians', and thus became some of the first (eighth century BCE) to use a form of writing that was simpler and more adaptable than the earlier cuneiform symbols. Once they took from the Phoenician playbook the idea of letters that suggested sounds and not concepts, they were off and writing—everything. This included stories heretofore known only orally, among them those many mythologies that might come close to Norris's idea of eternal.

"Writing gave Greeks the chance to approach their old myths with a new reflexive stance," explains the information architect Alex Wright in *Glut*. "Once the text became externalized, it could be subjected to analytical thought, reworked, and even improved on." Now we know why many of us get that proclivity to "put something down on paper."

And in case someone asks what purpose Greek *really* serves, here's something to chew on, courtesy of our *Glut* guru: "The interpolation of oral and literature cultures was the essential factor in the Greek contribution to human knowledge."

And with words that make us sound pretty darn smart.

## Making the Romans more like the Greeks

Those ever-pragmatic Romans knew a good idea when they had a chance to poach one. Put too simply: if the ancient Romans, with their massive legions, skewed toward brawn, the Greeks, with their dramas and poetry and mathematics and philosophy, skewed toward brain. By the first century BCE, elite Latin-speaking Romans were dropping Greek words into their conversations. And you can probably guess whose alphabet the Romans based theirs on.

Latin was long a vector for Greek. Before Mark Antony had him murdered in 43 BCE, the Roman statesman Cicero was a prolific translator of Greek texts into Latin. In doing so, he was making the neoteric concept of philosophy accessible to people for whom Greek was—well, Greek to them.

Cicero and other translators like Lucretius felt the Romans needed to up their ethical game. (Apparently Mark A. didn't get that memo.) The goal, as the classics professor Caryn Lehoux explains, was to create "a new kind of Roman self-image, one that actively cultivated political virtue over financial gain." According to Professor Carlos Lévy of the Sorbonne, Cicero had a clear agenda: "He wanted to extend the supremacy of Rome to an area formerly reserved to the Greeks."

Cicero was no *paganus*, that's for sure—although the Greeks went one better than *paganus* with their *barbaros*. The word suggested a strangeness coupled with ignorance. The plural, *barbaroi*, meant anybody who was not one of them—not a Greek. That made the person, as you've no doubt guessed, a **barbarian.** It's one of the Greeks' spell-it-like-the-sound-of-it, onomatopoeic words. As far as they were concerned, someone who could not speak Greek was just uttering a bunch of blah-blah-blah that to their ears sounded like *bar-bar-bar*. That included those Romans. And it was not just people that qualified for the label; so did a certain plant the Greeks called *rha barbaron*, which, being from China, was not one of theirs. We know it as **rhubarb**.

## From fables to philosophy

High-minded Ciceronian tomes weren't the only Greek works to be translated. Ross King, the cultural and art historian who wrote *Leonardo and the Last Supper* and *The Fantasia of Leonardo da Vinci*, tells us that among the translations that found their way onto Leonardo's bookshelf were the stories of that famous Greek fabulist Aesop. This was centuries after Aesop's death—the world had left the BCE calendar behind and was into the 1500s CE.

If you've ever **panicked**, suffered from **echolalia** (as Einstein did), become **furious**, struggled with a **phobia**, or been **tantalized,** blame it on some of those Greek gods—at least as far as word derivation. The guilty parties: Pan, Echo, Furies, Phobos, Tantalus.

Moreover, long after the ancient worlds of both Greece and Rome faded, Greek philosophy continues to endure. So have many lofty words English absorbed from those high-minded Hellenes. When Tom Morris is preparing a talk on a subject—failure, hope, virtue—he first researches the word's origin. It frequently takes him on his own etymological odyssey, from English through Latin to Greek.

"A lot of human wisdom is encoded in the history of words," he says. "When you view the concept of excellence, or the concept of virtue, through this history of Greek into Latin into English, you see a clustering of concepts. Maybe they saw something really important about relationships between ethics and excellence and power."

## Cosmic Milk

How is it that the English word **galaxy** derives from the Greek word (*gala*) for "milk"? Thank Hera, the goddess of childbirth. She missed the mark breastfeeding and created that distinctive grouping of bright stars we call the Milky Way. You can't make this stuff up. Unless, of course, you're an ancient Greek.

## The Woolf at Greek's Door

For centuries, anybody who was anybody in England's sphere of the learned, especially during the Victorian era, knew Greek. Let's qualify that: anybody who was anybody who was male. Then along came Virginia Woolf (1882–1941).

She decided at the age of fifteen that she was going to learn Greek. Since she couldn't study it formally—simply because she was a she—Woolf home-schooled herself. Greek translations, in Woolf's estimation, couldn't capture the language in its fullness.

In her 1925 essay "On Not Knowing Greek," she wrote:

> In spite of the labour and the difficulty it is this that draws us back and back to the Greeks; the stable, the permanent, the original human being is to be found there.

## How to Talk Like a Highfalutin Hellene

If you're in medicine, you use terms containing *gynec, cardia, ophthalmos, pneuma, derma*. The same holds true for the biological sciences: *stoma, schema, taxon, kytos, phyllo, phyto*. Mathematicians may know that **arithmetic, geometry, hyperbola, pentagon, parabola**—to count off a few—all derive from Greek.

What they might not know is that "parabola" is the source for **parable**, both coming from the Greek word for "juxtaposition." (Every now and then, you just have to go with what the etymology dishes up. And yes, **etymology** is from the Greek *etymos,* meaning "true.") Same deal with "hyperbola" and **hyperbole.**

If you've studied any Greek drama, these words might take you back to that classroom: *kathairein, hybris, hamartanein, theos ek mēchanēs, páthos.* In English:

- **catharsis** (purge)
- **hubris** (insolence leading to cockiness)
- **hamartia** (so far off the mark it's a fatal flaw—like hubris)
- **deus ex machina** (well, almost English—literally, "a god from a machine," making it a contrived exit when there's no other way)
- **pathos** (evoking pity). *Páthos* also shares the stage with **sympathy, apathy, empathy,** and **antipathy.**

So . . . given that you already know more Greek than you may have known you did, here are five higher-falutin Hellenisms to start tossing into conversations:

1. **phronesis:** practical wisdom
2. **synecdoche:** verbal shorthand—e.g., "suits" when referring to businesspeople
3. **propaedeutic:** preliminary study
4. **choropleth:** a map whose colored-in areas correspond to data values
5. **triskaidekaphobia:** fear (phobia) of the number 13

# 'Hysterical' May Not Be So Funny After All

When something is really, really funny, we're apt to say it's hysterical. But at the risk of sounding like a killjoy, there's really nothing funny about hysterics. For too long a time, it was known as "mother-sickness."

Whoa, where did *that* come from? From the Greek *hystera,* meaning "womb." As Maya Salam of *The New York Times* said in her review of Rachel Gross's book *Vagina Obscura,* the term "has been used to degrade women for centuries." Doctors treating women who suffered from maladies that men did not (or did not appear to) could point the finger at a faulty uterus.

Actually, the finger points to Hippocrates. Back in the fifth century BCE, the Greek physician was the first to use the term "hysterics" and to indicate a malfunctioning uterus as the cause.

The Hippocratic Oath that doctors still take, pledging to "first, do no harm," is noble. But the Hippocratic Oops, that women's illnesses occurred because they had that organ that went haywire and caused hysterics—that did considerable harm.

When something's really, really funny, try **hilarious** instead. It's from the Greek word for "cheerful."

## Q: What Do a Seahorse, Your Brain, and an Internal Combustion Engine Have in Common?

## A: *Hippo.*

Yes, the same *hippo* as in "hippopotamus," one of several unexpected creatures found in ancient Greece. *Potamos* refers to a river, and *hippos* refers to a horse: thus, a riverine horse.

The seahorse, which is a fish and not a horse, and which gets to be a foot long if it's lucky, nevertheless was once called a **hippocampus**. The *kampos* indicates a sea monster. That monstrous hippocampus in your head is a part of the brain that resembles a seahorse.

As for the internal combustion engine—the Belgian-French engineer who developed it in the mid-nineteenth century placed it in a three-wheeled carriage he built. It was actually a tricycle supporting a wagon that in turn held the engine. He called his horseless contraption, improbably, the Hippomobile.

## Utopia No More?

It's not exactly a toe-tapping title for a book: *Libellus vere aureus nec Minus Salutaris Quam Festivus de optimo reip. statu, deq; nova Insula Utopia.* But in the early sixteenth century, when it was published in England during the reign of Henry VIII, it was a hot property. The author was Sir Thomas More, Henry's future chancellor of England.

The New York Public Library counts among its treasures a first edition of the book, whose title a modern-day publisher would probably whack to just the final word: *Utopia.* Thomas More coined the word, borrowing not from the Latin in the rest of the title but from the Greek. As the Library explains, "the name 'utopia' derives from two identically pronounced Greek words: *eu-topos* (meaning 'good place') and *ou-topos* (meaning 'no place' or 'nowhere')."

More was writing about what a perfect society would look like. He even included a twenty-two-letter Utopian alphabet. But by naming this imaginary place Utopia, he was leaving it to history to decide whether he really believed in it or was slyly lampooning the idea.

More himself would soon be living in the opposite of a utopia: a **dystopia.** The word appeared much later, the "dys" signaling "bad," and things did indeed go badly for him. Henry had him beheaded after accusing him of treason. Hardly a utopian state of affairs.

## Greek, Game-Show Style

For these five clues, select the English word derived from Greek that matches the definition. Here are the words: **nostalgia, amethyst, nausea, eucharist, hermit.**

**Clue #1:** This has all the makings of an infomercial: "Ancient remedy that kept Dionysius, the god of wine, from getting drunk can do the same for you! Call now and ask for the word derived from the Greek for 'not intoxicated.'"

**Clue #2:** It's steeped in Christian religion, bound up with sacrament, ceremony, rite, and ritual. The word "consecration" often accompanies it. For all of this, it's a word that we could, um, resurrect for daily conversation, as it's all about gratitude and giving thanks.

**Clue #3:** What do you get when you mix the Greek *nostos* with *algos*? Broad hint: *nostos* means "return home" and *algos* means "pain." If you guessed "homesick," *ding ding ding:* you're right! Or at least, as far as the initial meaning. It is, after all, something Odysseus was on unhappy terms with, so no wonder Greek owns it. Eventually, though, one longing led to another, and before you knew it, the word held this broader meaning.

**Clue #4:** See also "anchorite" and "eremite." If you're a Star Wars fan, you're probably already there as far as the answer. If not, rather than propelling yourself into that galaxy far, far away, plunk yourself down in a desert—in Greek, *erēmia*—from long, long ago. Possibly you're fleeing something, most probably religious persecution. Such was the case for Paul of Thebes, who disappeared, alone, into the Egyptian desert around 250 CE. And in the desert he remained. He became the first Christian to be called this word.

**Clue #5:** Really broad hint: "nautical" and "nautilus" are first cousins of this word. Ancient seafarers succumbed to it. Then again, modern seafarers do, too—along with many landlubbers.

**Answers:** 1. amethyst, 2. eucharist, 3. nostalgia, 4. hermit, 5. nausea.

## Why *Do* We Say "It's Greek to Me"?

Why not "It's Archi to me"? Only a few thousand people speak Archi, and most of them live in the remote Russian village of Archib. Now, that's the way to drive home the point that you don't understand something.

That's not, however, how Shakespeare said it, and although he was not the first, he's the reason it stuck. In part, because of how cleverly he uses the common refrain in *Julius Caesar*.

In the play, Casca, soon to be one of Caesar's assassins, has just come from listening to our friend Cicero deliver an oration in Greek. Casca doesn't speak that language, and so his line of "It's Greek to me" becomes a double-entendre.

But if you do speak Greek, what comparable idiom might you reach for? Dan Nosowitz, writing in Atlas Obscura, offers this one: "To me, this appears like Chinese."

# 9.
# BONJOUR, BAYEUX: ENGLISH CHANNELS FRENCH

In 1016, the Viking king Cnut became king of all England—ruling over both the Danes, aka Vikings, in northeast England and the English in the rest of the country. It was big news at the time, but these days Cnut might be better remembered for who his grandfather was. Sure, gramps was the Danish king who united parts of Scandinavia. But that paled against his tooth color. The story goes that he had a blackish-blue tooth, from either too many blueberries or too little brushing. Thus his name of Harald Bluetooth, the inspiration for the name of today's technology that unites devices wirelessly.

Fifty years later, on the other hand, a Norman from France defeated the English king Harold at Hastings, on England's southeast coast. Just try to find an English person who doesn't have the name William the Conqueror and the year 1066 imprinted on their brain.

France's Normandy region is just across the channel that both connects and divides England and France. There must have been a hint of déjà vu in the Norman rout, given that William was of Viking descent (*"Oh no, this again . . . "*). Apparently, he and his Norsemen Normans hadn't lost their raiding touch.

"The invasion and conquest of the country by the Normans must rank as among the most complete and ruthless that any nation has had the misfortune to suffer," observes the historian Andrew Bridgeford in his book *1066: The Hidden History in the Bayeux Tapestry*.

To be fair, William was hardly an arriviste. He had been handpicked by the late English king, who was also his cousin, to be his successor. But Harold preempted him. Alas, Harold ended up swapping the crown on his head for an arrow near his eye at the decisive Battle of Hastings, becoming its most celebrated casualty. The 231-foot-long pictorial retelling of the battle known as the Bayeux Tapestry illustrates the moment. A Norman warrior then finishes the job, killing Harold with a well-placed sweep of his sword.

"At a stroke," writes Bridgeford, "the old English language became the tongue of the powerless underlings and it ceased largely . . . to be written down."

## Bid *Beowulf* adieu

The Norman French influence on England is indelible, thanks to the castles and cathedrals they built and that still stand. Those took some years to complete, but it took the French language no time at all to become the tongue that everybody who was anybody—namely, the French ruling elite—used. Azhar Alkazwini, writing in the *International Journal of Linguistics,* points out that "most of the vocabulary was considered 'exotic', as it was used in exclusive circles when dealing with matters of law, the church, and the running of country estates."

Over centuries the scope widened considerably, such that "a working knowledge of French for daily business dealings was far from being the preserve of the ruling elite," according to the late William Rothwell, the longtime general editor of the *Anglo-Norman Dictionary*. Eventually, more than just the Norman brand of French became the basis for approximately a third of English vocabulary.

And if we can simplistically say that Greek made English sound smart, French gave it a certain élan, making it sound elegant. Where the English tongue was more forthright, the French was more flowery. English had a king; French had a sovereign. The English ate sheep, cows, and deer; the French dined on mutton, beef, and venison. As R.J. White of Cambridge University put it: "The very language of government and administration, and soon of literature itself, lost much of its Saxon rudeness and flowed along in the more polite forms of Norman French."

Not that French has always hit it out of the park with the mot juste. Alexis de Tocqueville, France's extraordinarily prescient chronicler of American democracy in the eighteenth century, kept a diary—in French, of course—of his time in America. When he embarked for about two weeks into the American frontier, which started roughly at Saginaw, Michigan, the best French word he could find to describe it was *le désert*—the desert. Americans, thanks to the Beowulf boys, had a better word. In fact, it was one that the Puritan William Bradford, not long after alighting from the *Mayflower*, used to describe America: wilderness.

## Guess what conquered the Conqueror?

Back to the Bayeux boys.

After William quite literally crushed it at Hastings, he headed north and decimated more of the populace. Oddly, he did not do the same with the language. In fact, he tried to learn it.

But it seems that, while William conquered England, English vanquished him. It was just too hard for him to learn. It would be more than three hundred years before the first language of an English king was English.

English was what the French elite of William's time might have called déclassé. Nevertheless, the working-class tongue held on. The common folk of England continued to speak it, and by the 1400s, it was pretty well understood that English was the spoken language, while French and Latin functioned as written ones. In effect, the country became trilingual.

Even so, the impact of French on the native tongue was as irreversible as the sword that pierced Harold. As James D. Gordon wrote in *The English Language: An Historical Introduction,* "the changes that occurred after the Norman Conquest were more radical than in any other period of which we have historical knowledge."

(To wit: for this chapter, we owe a debt to French for not only "bonjour" and "adieu" but also **déjà vu**, **élan**, **mot juste**, **arriviste**, and **déclassé**—and those are just the obvious ones.)

## Let's Have a Turn at Trilingualism

French often serves as a kind of linguistic water bearer of Latin. Lots of words that originated in Latin found their way into English through French. That's the case for this A-to-V listing (minus K, which *was* an arriviste). But here's the kicker: these are all French spellings. And there are more where these came from.

While it's a fairly easy leap to see how the French *antiquitet, calamité,* and *estremité* became the English **antiquity**, **calamity**, and **extremity**, the Latin-to-French words that follow require nary a nudge, let alone a leap, to recognize in English. And the meanings are similar. One caveat: French pronunciation would, of course, be different.

*absence . . . brutal . . . calorie . . . diatribe . . . ellipse . . . flexible . . . glacial . . . habitable . . . illusion . . . juxtaposition . . . large . . . menace . . . notable . . . ogre . . . passage . . . quadrant . . . risible . . . scorpion . . . torrent . . . union . . . verisimilitude*

## A Double Dip of Legalese

Why do attorneys use phrases like "will and testament" and "goods and chattels"? Aren't these and other such conjoinings a tad repetitive? Maybe, but this is a case where redundancy ensures clarity. They're known as doublets, and you can thank our 1066 Man of the Year for many of them.

William's conquest coincided roughly with the beginnings of England's common-law system of justice. While barristers would be writing the law in French, they would be administering it to a citizenry that understood only English. The double-duty wording was a nod to both languages.

Thus the English "will" pairs with the French and Latin "testament," and the English "goods" with the French "chattels."

We can also thank the French for **bail**, another Latin derivative that became the Old French *baillier*. The word means to guard or deliver, as in handing over the bond money, or bail, that springs someone from jail. (**Bailiff** springs from a comparable source.) Old French also gave us the forerunner of **jail**: *jaiole*.

## *Paganus* Is Back, So Mind Those Sabotaging Shoes

This time our much maligned *paganus* appears as *paisant,* which in English would eventually become **peasant.** *Paisant,* in Old French, indicated one of the locals, the *pais* meaning "country." But the country eventually came to the city, and the result was **sabotage**.

The root is *sabot,* French for the wooden shoes that peasants throughout Europe wore. When the Industrial Revolution brought those shod in *sabots* from the country to the cities and into the factories to work, they were often all thumbs at the job, slowing down production. Plus, their shoes made a racket.

Toward the end of the nineteenth century, when French labor unions held work slowdowns, they referred to them as *sabotage* (another French word you already knew). Today the term applies to all kinds of undermining and disruptions, no clumsy *sabots* required.

## What "Queue" Takes Its Cue From

"Queue," those lines of people that the British are famous for not jumping, takes its cue etymologically from *cue,* the Old French word for an animal's tail. Why the Brits added all those extra letters is a mystery, but the reference to a tail is not.

"When the noun showed up in English in the 16th century, it meant a tail-like band of parchment used to seal a letter," the *Grammarphobia* team of Patricia T. O'Conner and Stuart Kellerman tell us in their blog. It would take another four centuries for "queue" as we now use it to appear, and first as a verb. Perhaps because when you first queue, you're at the tail end of the line . . . ?

Knowing the role that "tail" plays in the term, it follows that the single plait of hair that Chinese males were at one time required to wear, and that resembled what some might call a pigtail, was called a "queue."

## Four French Words That Jumped the Queue

These words took a detour in meaning when they got to English:

1. *Gentil* gave us **genteel**, but also **jaunty**, a later arrival that added a spring in the step of the more refined "genteel."

2. *Étiquette* gave us the same word in English (sans accent), with the same meaning, but also **ticket**. Actually, before the word came to mean the practice of good manners, the first French meaning was "ticket."

3. *Traison* gave us **treason** but also **tradition**. Thank the Latin *traditio* for this. Its verb form, *tradere,* means to hand over. One hands over, or down, a tradition, and also hands over harmful information that can result in treason.

4. *Gargole* gave us **gargoyle** but also **gargle**. The purpose of the French architectural element called a gargoyle was to act as a type of gutter on buildings. The gargoyle funneled water through the creature's "throat"—which is the original meaning of *gargole*.

## True or False? The French Word *Mayonnaise* Comes From:

a. The Seven Years' War, when the French seized the British port of Mahon (which had been Spain's) and liberated the precursor to mayonnaise, a sauce named for this Mediterranean city: *mahonesa*.
b. The French *manier*, meaning "to stir," which one does when making mayo from scratch (don't even whisper *Miracle Whip* to this cohort).
c. The French *moyeu,* or egg yolk, a common ingredient.
d. The French town of Bayonne, because, as a nineteenth-century French chef observed, the town "contains many inventive gourmands."
e. All of the above, or none of the above.

As Sam Dean wrote in the *Bon Appétit* blog where he put forth all these possibilities, mayonnaise remains "a condiment as historically complicated as it is delicious." Choose e, and you mayo be right.

## A Gallant Mashup

Fittingly, **cuisine** is from the French; originally it meant kitchen. But here's a French food term that you're not likely to find in any kitchen: **gallimaufry.**

The *Oxford English Dictionary* has described it as "a dish made by hashing up odds and ends of food." The Old French *galimafree* hints at a stew or a sauce. Might the main ingredient in that word be *galer,* from which we get **gallant**? Perhaps those who endured eating this hash-up mashup were just being polite.

You rarely find gallimaufry describing a food dish now, so don't look for it in your favorite neighborhood restaurant. (Also fittingly, **restaurant** is from the French; originally it meant to restore or refresh, which a good restaurant still does.) These days, "gallimaufry" has become a way to dish on a figurative hodgepodge, like a random collection of essays. It is, in fact, the French word that the sixteenth-century English poet Edmund Spenser chose when bemoaning what he saw as the hodgepodging (just made that up) of the English language: "So now they have made our English tongue a gallimaufry . . . of all other speeches." Think he saw the irony?

## The French Connection

American Sign Language, or ASL, is a distinct language from English. In fact, Gallaudet University in Washington, DC, the world's only liberal arts university for deaf and hard of hearing students, offers an ASL and English Bilingualism program.

One of the first influences on the development of ASL in the early nineteenth century was *langue des signes française:* French Sign Language. Americans had no experience at the time in deaf communication, so Thomas Hopkins Gallaudet traveled to Europe to learn from French teachers who were already schooled in successful signing for the deaf.

## Oh, No, It's (sort of) Faux!

The French language has that *je ne sais quoi,* or certain something, that is often irresistible to English speakers. Consider how natural these French expressions sound to many of us. Except that . . . one of them is an impostor. Can you spot it?

*amuse-bouche*
*c'est la vie*
*carte blanche*
*force majeure*
*joie de vivre*
*noblesse oblige*
*nom de plume*

The dissembler in our midst, the language mavens Patricia T. O'Conner and Stewart Kellerman tell us, is *nom de plume*. Granted, the words are French—*nom* meaning name and *plume* meaning feather, whose quill, when dipped in ink, once served as a writing instrument. While we know this as "pen name" in English, O'Conner and Kellerman maintain that "*nom de plume* is not an old French expression—or a new one, either. The British made it up."

The correct French expression, they advise, is **nom de guerre**—literally, "war name." A Victorian novelist whom nobody remembers swapped out "war" for "feather" in the mid-nineteenth century, and it stuck.

# 10.
# WHY CAN'T THE ENGLISH TEACH THEIR CHILDREN HOW TO SPELL?

Since 1925, the annual Scripps National Spelling Bee has been causing sweaty palms among young students in America as contestants verbally duke it out, letter by letter, in this heavyweight of spelling competitions. *Fracas* (1930). *Semaphore* (1946). *Insouciant* (1951). *Sycophant* (1964). *Autochthonous* (2004). And these aren't even the most obscure words, just a handful of the "winning" ones.

*Ironic* has not yet made that list, but it is a word that aptly describes holding spelling bees on the English language. By their nature, these competitions imply that the spelling of a word is immutable. But doesn't that suggest that there's some *logic* to the spelling?

As if.

As the polyglot Gaston Dorren observes about the English language in his book *Babel*, "The spelling is infamous for its idiosyncratic and whimsical relation to pronunciation."

But the poets sometimes like it.

## An ordered disorder, somewhat

The fictional professor Henry Higgins of *My Fair Lady*, which is set in twentieth-century Edwardian England, famously bemoaned English children's inability to speak properly (upper-crust code for "kill the Cockney accent"). He may well have sung a similar lament about English spelling, which can seem to resemble chaos theory. Yet the spelling actually follows some specific patterns that pay homage, in their own convoluted way, to the many different languages that have influenced English.

Had the early speakers of Germanic languages, among others, never wanted to write things down, we wouldn't be having this conversation about spelling. But fortunately they did. Their early Runic alphabet, consisting of symbols cast in straight lines, was conducive to carving in wood but not composing on vellum. Eventually it got edged out by the Roman alphabet, which, like much of early Roman literature, got its start with the Greek.

That was hardly the end of the Roman influence on English spelling, as the linguistics professor David Crystal points out. Crystal is a recipient of the Order of the British Empire for his work with the English language. It could be argued that he deserves an even higher honor for writing *Spell It Out: The Curious, Enthralling and Extraordinary Story of English Spelling.* Those qualities the story may be, but it's also the kind of twisted, tortuous tale that, as a friend is fond of saying, makes your hair hurt. Think about it for a moment: from what fresh orthographic hell does **rhapsodic** spring? (Thank the ancient Greeks and their *rhapsōidia*, a word reserved for reciting epic poems. It was possible to get a job in those days as a rhapsode, recounting these poems. No spelling skills needed.)

It's doubtful, though, that Crystal would agree about either the hurting hair or hell. "I have wanted to write a book on English spelling all my life," he tells us at the very beginning of his book,

> but the prospect has always scared me. There is simply so much of it. . . . the task of attempting to find some order in the chaos . . . seemed well-nigh impossible.

It's hardly a spoiler to learn that Crystal does, indeed, identify order in the disorder. Here are a few of the broad strokes.

Some of the apparent disconnect between spelling and saying is due to the inherent sponginess of English, its penchant for soaking up words from other languages, all of which have their own spelling conventions. For example, the English love affair for all words Latin, in full flower by the 1500s, provided a wealth of words for English to adopt. Never mind whatever spelling conventions may already have been in place for English: when in the Romans' language, spell as the Latin does. Thus, as Crystal demonstrates, we are "timid" rather than "timmid," which would have been the English spelling and pronunciation at the time. But the Latin was *timulus.*

The same held true of French-origin words. The scribes of William the Conqueror tossed out those *foreign*-looking Anglo-Saxon letters for the Roman ones they favored. They also spruced up spellings so they were more to their liking: *service,* for example, not *servis.* Never mind that *servis* had better served phonetically.

When William Caxton introduced the printing press to England in the latter half of the fifteenth century, he decided to spell the way the English in London and southeast England spoke. It was a step toward standardization, but with an unintended consequence: codifying the spelling's hot mess. "It is to this that English owes some of its chaotic and exasperating spelling conventions," maintain McCrum, Cran, and MacNeil.

Then there was the influence of the Great Vowel Shift that occurred from roughly the fifteenth to seventeenth centuries. Though not exclusive to English, its impact on spelling was manifold. Very simplistically put, people started to talk differently because they changed how they pronounced long vowels. This altered some spellings, though not all—remember: do not seek consistency and logic in this tale.

As James Gleick describes it in *The Information*, this was the sixteenth-century state of spelling affairs: "Every time people dipped quill in ink to form a word on paper they made a fresh choice of whatever letters seemed to suit the task."

## Encore to the Revolution

By the eighteenth century, there were now upstarts across the Pond who were also mucking things up. Noah Webster was notable among these Americans. He was a keen admirer of Benjamin Franklin, who had tried his own hand at simplifying English's spelling. Webster proved the more successful.

In 1783, the year the American Revolution ended, Webster started his own little revolution with the publication of *The American Spelling Book*. He was still at it decades later, citing "the evil of our irregular orthography," which he deemed "barbarous." He followed his speller in 1828 with *An American Dictionary of the English Language*. Webster was, as his biographer Harlow Giles Unger tells us, "the last lexicographer ever to write an entire dictionary... with no help." Like Samuel Johnson, whose 1755 dictionary was also a one-man show, he supplemented the definition of words with quotes by famous people to illustrate their meaning, tapping American personages such as George Washington and Washington Irving.

"Webster was a better definer than Johnson: less literary, but more exact," according to *The New Yorker* regular Jill Lepore. Ah, but that *spelling*. It met with opprobrium on both sides of the Pond for wanting to make English less English ("perfectly absurd to talk of the *American* language," sniffed one newspaper editor in, ironically, Philadelphia, where the American patriot Benjamin Franklin had earlier been the publisher of the *Pennsylvania Gazette*).

Nevertheless, Webster's dictionary is why we spell it "music" and not "musick" (the Brits were fond of appending a k to any word that would otherwise have ended with a c). And of course, it's why Americans have "humor" instead of "humour," although the British were not amused that their spelling was being abused. Along with changing many "ou" spellings to just "o," Webster ousted the second l out of some words, like "traveller," but then added a second l to others, like "appal."

It wasn't all smooth skating. He tried to change "prove" to "proov," one of many orthographic challenges he lost. Which just goes to proov that even seemingly random spelling has its standards.

## Et Tu, Claudius?

Even Latin, one of the presumed culprits of English's capricious spelling, had its own would-be reformers. The Roman emperor Claudius (10 BCE –54 CE) tried to make some spelling changes, with little success.

As for *materia,* the word for timber that we met back in the PIE days (chapter 2), that was how ancient Romans like Claudius would have known, and spelled, the word. By the Middle Ages, as Ross King tells us, the word had morphed into *materiamen*—and gained fifty different spellings. Maybe we got it from these guys.

## And You as Well, George?

It turns out that Henry Higgins did grouse about how the English spelled, in a roundabout way. It was actually the playwright George Bernard Shaw, creator of *Pygmalion*, the inspiration for *My Fair Lady*. Shaw, who died in 1950, made simpler spelling a cause he took to his grave and left in his will. He railed against an alphabet too puny for the job and maintained that "the English language cannot be spelt with five Latin vowels."

## How to Be Right Even When They Say Your Spelling Is Wrong

Today we know that "right" means one thing, "write" another, and "rite" something else entirely, even though we pronounce all three the same way. Right?

But as Merriam-Webster's lexicographer Kory Stamper tells us in *Word by Word*, back in the fifteenth century, you could have chosen any of seventy-seven different ways to spell "right" and you would have been *reyt*. Also *rith*. And *rycht, rethe, rigt*. And so on.

Seventy-seven ways to be "right" was hardly a rarity. Melvyn Bragg, in his *Adventure of English*, tells us that "through" once had—wait for it—five hundred spellings. Even the deceptively simple, straightforward "she" had more than sixty.

## Pop Quiz: How Many English Words Spelled With 'Eak' at the End Rhyme With 'Break'?

Answer: One, according to David Crystal (who's gonna argue with an OBE?). "Let them eat . . . steak."

The spelling is in part the result of "stake" already being taken by the time this meat became popular in the fifteenth century. It's also an example of one of myriad reasons for the vagaries of English spelling—to distinguish one word from another that sounded like it.

## Ugh, Ugh, Ugh: This Chameleon Changes Its Sound

*Bough, though, tough, through, cough, brought*: just hearing u-g-h words in English gives someone new to the language low odds that they'll spell them correctly. It's what British-born Polly Barton, a Japanese/English translator, calls "the hellish unpredictability of English pronunciation."

Could that be why, in many instances today, we've taken the "ugh" out of "doughnut," to render "donut"? (We're talkin' to you, Dunkin'.) Behold: an English word that's spelled the way it's pronounced, and pronounced the way it's spelled! Somewhat surprisingly, Noah Webster had his chance to be the hero with this one but passed. In his *American*

*Dictionary of the English Language,* he presents it as dough-nut. (This was back when "nut" described a small, round cake.)

## Why Can't the English Teach Their Children How to Spell Like Spanish?

You might think that with all the influence Spanish has had on English, at least American English, we would have taken our spelling cue from *español.* Spain did, after all, control a significant chunk of what became the US at least one hundred fifty years before the English moved in.

Spanish spelling is pretty much what-you-see-is-what-you-say, and always the same way: the sound of each letter of the alphabet, or pairings of letters, is breathtakingly consistent. Moreover, all but one letter in a word is pronounced, "h" for the most part remaining mum. Ironically, this say-it-as-you-see-it convention was true of Old English, so a word like "hope" would have been pronounced something like "ho-puh." But all such ho-puh of English pronunciation staying that way was dashed, as the language continued its ineluctable march toward making every language it collided with part of its own.

# 11. ROMANCING THE RENAISSANCE

Overheard in Anthony Doerr's epic, and epoch-spanning, novel *Cloud Cuckoo Land:*

> "Boil the words you already know down to their bones," Rex says, "and usually you'll find the ancients sitting there at the bottom of the pot, staring back up."

As early as the 1400s, a "reanimation of antiquity," as Ross King so artfully describes it in *The Bookseller of Florence,* was taking place in Europe. "Italian writers began using the word *rinascita* to express this extraordinary efflorescence of culture," he writes.

While this **Renaissance**, as we would come to know it (fittingly, from the Latin *re,* meaning "again," plus *nascere,* "to be born") manifested itself in different ways and at different times throughout Europe, the advent of Gutenberg's printing press in 1454 was a catalyst. King relays how one admirer of the new invention gleefully thumbed his nose at handwritten books, in verse: "For what a quill can write the whole year through,/This in a day, and more, his press will do."

Not to be outdone by Gutenberg's invention, England boasted its own printing press less than twenty years later, thanks to William

Caxton. His version of "This in a day" was a history of Troy: the first book in English to come off a printing press. But it hadn't been written originally in English—this was Caxton's translation from the French.

## Exponential English

By the sixteenth century, the English language was becoming more expansive, thanks to its citizens becoming more enlightened. More books led to more knowledge, and more knowledge to more words.

Always before, the English language had grown primarily by the country that was invading it—the Angles and the Saxons, the Jutes and the Frisians, the Romans, the Vikings, the Normans. As far as French, however, the Normans hardly had the last words. To the thousands already installed in the English language would come thousands more. This time the words originated in central France and, importantly, Paris, a shift that had begun in the thirteenth century. Parisian French became *de rigueur,* no sword needed.

A certain adventure at sea would also eventually lead to English becoming awash in words. In 1588 England repulsed the invasion of the Spanish Armada, a fleet of warships also known, ironically, as the Invincible Armada—**armada** deriving from the Latin for "to equip or arm." After that, England's naval presence was formidable, not just for fighting but for trading. For the English language, the victory was akin to winning the Lexical Lotto.

## Of sailors and scholars

"As England imported a huge cargo of goods, English imported a huge cargo of vocabulary," observes Bragg. Language historians put the cache of new words that piled up over the ensuing years at ten thousand, easy. They ranged from the more sedate **explore** and **embargo** to the more adventurous **smuggle** and **desperado.**

It was not uncommon for words in Dutch, Portuguese, and Italian to make their way back to England on its trade ships. "Sailors were the messengers of language," as McCrum, Cran, and MacNeil describe it.

If the sailor was the messenger, the learned class was the maker. Science and its new discoveries were moving knowledge forward, prompting philosophers and scholars to look backwards to languages that seemed better equipped to express such concepts as *atmosphere* and *gravity*. Their languages of choice? Some Greek, of course, and definitely Latin.

It wasn't an entirely new idea. An eleventh-century scholar wrote the definitive recounting of the voyages of the Norse in Latin; he was German. Thomas Thomas's 1587 *Dictionarium*, a Latin-English dictionary, sought to explain English vocabulary in Latin. James Gleick, who wrote of this in *The Information,* tells us that "mapping Latin onto English made a kind of sense that translating English to English did not."

## A Renaissance redux, redux

Twice before in England, when Latin had been the language in charge, the Romans had been right there, either with the soldiers of Claudius expanding an empire or the soldiers of Christ spreading their new religion. This third time proved to be the charm. Ironically, it seems the Romans' language had the greatest effect when the Romans themselves were in absentia.

For scholars throughout Europe, Latin became the lingua franca through which they could share ideas with one another. Besides, it made you sound smart. Mind you, this was none of that Latin for the masses. *This* Latin was, as King describes it, "the glorious language of Cicero." Throwing in some ancient Greek just added to the glory.

And so Isaac Newton wrote his *Philosophiae Naturalis Principia Mathematica* (*Mathematical Principles of Natural Philosophy*) in 1687 not in his native English, but in Latin. Galileo Galilei wrote his *Sidereus Nuncius* (*Starry Messenger*) in 1610 not in his native Italian, but in Latin. King estimates that over ninety percent of the books printed in Europe in the latter half of the fifteenth century were printed in Latin.

In addition, Greek was becoming more accessible. Many Greek scholars had fled west when the Turks overtook Constantinople (now Istanbul) in 1453, settling in Venice in particular. A printer there named

Aldus Manutius published their works, preserving the original Greek. Today, a devoted cohort of rare-book lovers still purchases his Aldine Press books. (Btw, *if you ever use italic type*, thank Aldus: his print shop invented it.)

## How do you say 'off the deep end' in Latin?

And then there was Shakespeare.

He was, of course, a key player in England's sixteenth- and seventeenth-century word fest, as we shall see in chapter 12. But despite reaching back to antiquity for some of his plays, and immortalizing the Latin *Et tu, Brute?* as Julius Caesar's dying words (even though Caesar's final words were probably uttered in Greek, the language of the nobility), Shakespeare wasn't all in when it came to a surfeit of this classical-language stuff. It did not go unnoticed.

When the playwright Ben Jonson eulogized his friend in 1623 in the preface to Shakespeare's First Folio, he offered due praise (mainly forgotten) and just the hint of a dig (well-remembered): "though thou hadst small Latine, and lesse Greeke, From thence to honour thee."

Oh well, fair Will, at least thou hadst that Dane.

Things got a little **extreme** (yep, Latin: *extremus*) with some of these classicists. Consider the seventeenth-century English poet John Dryden. Both the lexicographer Kory Stamper and the language historian Jack Lynch tell us how Dryden was so **smitten** (*not* Latin—from Old English *smitan*) with Latin that he would do a kind of reverse engineering with his writing: he would translate his English sentences into Latin, and then back into English, in an attempt to maintain the trappings of Latin grammar. You do that too, right?

Let's blame Dryden—keeping in mind that others were complicit—for that old chestnut about never ending a sentence with a preposition. That's trying to do unto English what's done in Latin. But English enjoys a kind of dual linguistic citizenship, with Germanic roots and Romance shoots. That preposition prohibition is something English speakers need not put up with.

# e pluribus ENGLISH

## It's inkhorn alright . . . but is it English?

Not every English speaker of the time was a Latin lover. McCrum, Cran, and MacNeil tell of one purist (a term we must take with several grains of salt when we're talking about English) who wanted to expunge the Latin-based *impenetrable*. His alternative: *ungothroughsome*.

Such an idea was, to purloin another of this purist's ineuphonious alternatives, *not-to-be-thought-upon-able*. (He must have somehow missed the Greek *euphonia,* as it's still humming along in modern dictionaries.)

This literal-to-the-letter does get your attention, though. Which may be why one testimonial for the 2022 history book *Black Snow* was simply a resounding "unputdownable." And in case it seems *inconceivable* (aka not-to-be-thought-upon-able) that this word would be in a dictionary, *Merriam-Webster* says it's been around since 1935.

On the flip side of *those* funny-sounding words were the numerous inkhorn words that, in the view of many, were Latin in extremis. "Inkhorn," or *blaechorn* in Old English, has a surprisingly straightforward meaning: ink that was carried in an animal's horn, much like gunpowder was carried in a powder horn. If you had the inky variety, odds are you were a scribe or scholar. The term morphed into a description of pretentious words, with Latinate ones taking the prize for pedantry.

In the abridged edition of Samuel Johnson's 1755 English dictionary edited by Jack Lynch, a professor of English and leading Johnson scholar, one of the longest entries in his index of piquant terms is for those deemed inkhorn. Some of them teeter on six syllables, give or take. And, while many in the original two-volume, two-thousand-page dictionary eventually went the way of actual inkhorns and powder horns, that's not the case for all. Others spawned progeny that have just a few minor changes in spelling.

*Flammivomous,* for example, which Johnson graphically defined as "vomiting out flame," is not in the online edition of *Merriam-Webster*, but *flammiferous* is, defined as "producing or bright with flame." *Rotundifolious* isn't there, either, but one might ask why not, since *asperifolious* is. *Merriam-Webster* defines that as "rough-leaved," the *asper* from whence we get **asperity.** Johnson defined *rotundifolious* as "having round leaves," an amalgam of the Latin for "round," from which we also get **rotunda**, and the Latin for "leaf" (think **foliage**).

## Those obstreperous Americans get into the act

This tug-of-war between two tongues—one more cerebral classical, the other more earthy native—continues, in one way or another, ad infinitum. If you were one of the privileged who skewed both cerebral and earthy, you were well-armed to jump into the fray. That was true on both sides of the Pond.

Samuel Adams (1722–1803), so dedicated to the cause of America's right to self-government that he makes his pal Paul Revere look like a patriotic slacker, was educated at Boston Latin before he headed to Harvard. Not surprisingly, Boston Latin's emphasis was on the classics. Adams performed well.

"Soon," his biographer Stacy Schiff tells us, "he began to fit Aesop's fables into Latin verse. Afterward came translations of Erasmus, submitted in English and rendered, at week's end, back into Latin." (Channeling Dryden, perhaps?)

As he helped push his country toward independence, Adams at one point flipped his classical training. He saw to it that the royal governor that Britain had installed in Massachusetts was challenged when, in 1773, the Brit insisted that Adams and his fellow colonial House members redo the legislative bills they had submitted.

As Schiff recounts, the governor, Thomas Hutchinson, enjoined that they be rewritten—in Latin. "What was so extraordinary, the House challenged Hutchinson, about plain English?" It was a shrewd way for Adams to attach Latin to the heavy-handed British, and English to a democratic American polity. Guess who won?

But just to add another twist, Schiff tells us that after those translations of Erasmus that Adams worked on at Boston Latin, "a steady stream of Ovid, Cicero, Virgil, and Homer followed, a reading list that imprinted itself, stylistically and substantively, in its accents and allusions, on the literature of the American Revolution." Just as the Romans drew from the Greek thinkers, the architects of the soon-to-be United States drew from them both.

## 'A third register'

Thanks to the Renaissance and what followed, it's safe to say that for the English language, the genie was out of the bottle. Or, to be Latin about it, *alea iacta est*. The die was, indeed, cast as far as English now having a plethora of those ancients stirring the linguistic pot, and the mix of Latin and Greek to what then constituted English made it all the more potent.

Kevin Stroud, in his *History of English* podcast, sums it up smartly:

> Whereas French loanwords had given English lots [of] synonyms and had effectively given English a second register above Old English, all of these new Latin and Greek words gave English a third register. It meant that English speakers were often given three different words to choose from—a basic and plain Germanic word from Old English or Old Norse, a slightly more elevated or posh word from French, and now an even more sophisticated or scholarly word from Latin or Greek.

As an example of the elementary to elegant to erudite, Stroud offers the Old English "think," the French "ponder," and the Latin "contemplate."

There was still plenty of room in the pot for more. English was set to absorb all kinds of other words from any number of places in the world. Flypaper might be more discriminating. But therein lies the power of letting language be language.

As Samuel Johnson (whom we'll hear from again in chapter 12) said of English, "attempts to enchain syllables" were as futile as those "to lash the wind."

## Honk If You've Heard This Inkhorn Before

Here are some of the Latin-based inkhorn words that appear in Samuel Johnson's 1755 dictionary, along with his definitions for each. Five of these words have disappeared from dictionaries—at least, from the online edition of *Merriam-Webster*. But seven of them have not. Can you guess which? Answers are at the end of the chapter.

1. aberuncate: "To pull up by the roots."
2. allubescency: "Willingness."
3. crepitate: "To make a small crackling noise."
4. excubation: "The act of watching all night."
5. gemelliparous: "Bearing twins."
6. immarcescible: "Unfading."
7. nullibiety: "The state of being nowhere."
8. salsamentarious: "Belonging to salt things."
9. stridulous: "Making a small noise."
10. stultiloquence: "Foolish talk."
11. tralatitious: "Metaphorical; not literal."
12. viduity: "Widowhood."

## More Dryden Channeling: A Famous Nom de Plume

Or *nom de guerre*, if we want to get technical. Watch how this name goes from English to Latin and back to English.

| | |
|---|---|
| His name was: | Charles Lutwidge Dodgson |
| He dropped the last name: | Charles Lutwidge |
| Translated the remaining two into Latin: | Carolus Ludovicus |

Reversed their order: . . . . . . . . . . . . . . . Ludovicus Carolus
And anglicized them: . . . . . . . . . . . . . . . . . Lewis Carroll

## In Case You Thought Latin Was Dead

"Status: Extinct." So say the creators of the language site The Language Gulper about Latin.

*Not so fast,* says John McWhorter—again. In answer to the question of why Latin died out as a language that many people spoke, McWhorter says, "it didn't—it slowly developed into a new language in the many places it spread."

This is by no means a diss on The Language Gulper. Besides having a clever name, the site provides an exhaustive overview of more than one hundred thirty languages. You can also get online lessons in Sanskrit— in either English or Spanish.

Besides, in addition to noting that Latin remains an official language of the Vatican, The Language Gulper actually lands on the same page as McWhorter as far as Latin's second chapter, noting that Latin "was the seed of the Romance languages."

That's a mighty powerful seed. While Latin is slathered all over English speakers' tongues derivatively (for the most part), it is the seed from which five national languages done sprung: Italian, Spanish, Portuguese, French, and (did you guess?) Romanian.

How on earth did that last one get in the group, you may wonder, since Romania is the Eastern European odd one out. It's because the Roman Empire looked both west and east, and in the second century, decided to add what is today Romania to its list of conquests.

Consider how similar these Spanish and Romanian words are, and there are many more just like these to Romance the two languages:

- *Diente* and *dinte* for tooth
- *Evitar* and *evita* for avoid
- *Fruta* and *fruct* for fruit
- *Largo* and *larg* for long
- *Mesa* and *masa* for table

More than nine hundred million speakers in the world now chatter away in a Romance language. And while English is considered a Germanic language (those Frisians at work), Guillaume the Conqueror and his Norman French entourage saw to it that there was plenty of Romance for English speakers.

As a bilingual friend whose first language is Spanish cleverly puts it, you would be dead wrong if you thought that Latin was dead. We give it mouth-to-mouth resuscitation every day.

## In Case You Think Latin Is Elitist

"Latin is often seen as a kind of elitist thing that only certain types of people have access to," said the classicist Jason Pedicone, the cofounder and president of the New York-based Paideia Institute for Humanistic Study, in an interview. (*Paideia* is from the Greek for education.) A Princeton PhD who speaks both Latin and Greek, Pedicone and his organization offer immersive language programs for students who can check the over-18 box. They study Greek in Greece and Latin in Rome and Paris. In Paris, the emphasis is on medieval Latin. During the Middle Ages, university students attending the Sorbonne in Paris studied in Latin—which is how that part of Paris came to be called the Latin Quarter.

But Paideia offers another Latin-language program that started in Brooklyn and is for younger students. Called Aequora, it's a free outreach program that uses Latin to improve English literacy for elementary and middle school students, particularly in communities whose schools do not offer Latin. Online offerings have included one that The New York Public Library hosted.

Pedicone vividly recalls the moment a fifth-grade Latina whose first language was Spanish realized that Spanish and English often had Latin in common. "The fact that she knew Spanish made her really good at Latin, actually gave her a leg up," Pedicone said. "The joy that she felt in that was pretty remarkable."

## Okay, Maybe a Little Elitist

Just pull this word out the next time you encounter a know-it-all who doesn't know it all: **ultracrepidarian**. It's loaded with Latin—*ultra*, meaning beyond; *crepida*, indicating footwear; and the expression *Ne supra crepidam sutor iudicaret*. The translation, according to Oxford Languages: "The cobbler should not judge beyond his shoe." Meaning: Don't try to be the expert in areas beyond your expertise.

## A Greek *Gotcha!*

Mention Greek, and many of us knee-jerk toward words like *onomatopoeia*: long, complex, with are-you-serious spellings. But here's a word from Greek that is just so darn simple. By more than coincidence, it shares part of the same word origin, meaning "to make," with *onomatopoeia* (the *poeia* part): **poet.** While "poetic" and "poetry" are neutral extensions of the word, Latin and French added a killjoy suffix that no person who makes poems wants to hear: *aster*. A **poetaster** is a second-rate poet. Or, as Samuel Johnson minced no words in defining it: "A vile petty poet."

## Latin Teaser: What's Small and Red, and Why Might That Be Redundant?

When medieval scribes were lettering certain important parts of a manuscript, such as a saint's feast day, they used red paint to help them stand out. We still acknowledge this custom when we refer to an event as a **red-letter day.**

As Ross King relays in *The Bookseller of Florence,* this lettering was a specialized skill that a *miniatore* would undertake. That Italian word was from the Latin *miniare,* "to color red." The term became linked with *miniatura,* or small in size, and gradually came to mean a work in **miniature.** The connection with a color disappeared. Fortunately, so did the lead base it was formulated from: it was poisonous.

 **Meanderthal Moment:** Many early Arabic books also featured this **rubrication** (Latin again, *rubrica,* meaning a red color), but for a different reason. As the social historian Judith Flanders tells us, even when books became plentiful, "the Arab world continued to regard memory as a primary tool of scholarship." Having lavishly decorated books that featured words inked in red helped Arab scholars file the material in memory.

## Mystery Histories

It helps to be a bit of a word masochist to wade into this quiz. For each of these word histories, guess the word(s) the stories describe.

1. "Aristotle minted the word *mollusk*—in the UK it's mollusc—from the Latin *mollis,* or soft, to describe fleshy bodies," the environmental journalist Cynthia Barnett tells us in *The Sound of the Sea.* While that usage refers to something physical, the root of "mollusk" also forms another word that's more abstract. Is it . . .

    **a. mellifluous     b. mufflec     c. mollify**

2. Greek gives us this word for using something old to identify something new. These are usually visual triggers, but they can also be acoustical. Take a photo with your cellphone and you might hear the whisper of a *click!* Use your cellphone to make a call and you tap

the image of a landline phone receiver. These cues can be the equivalent of comfort food for those who can recall the old-time sights and sounds. Is the word . . .

    **a. skewness**    **b. skeuomorph**    **c. skepsis**

3. Both these words share a common Greek root, and both have something to do with how we see the world. But from there they diverge, with the first borrowing from the German, and the second from the Latin and Greek.

First one: When we look at something and see something it is not, the first word is at work. An example: the rocky outcrops in Colorado Springs whose formations appear to be kissing camels (or so the locals will keep telling you).

Second one: The second word is frequently defined as an aberration of our vision. In his *Bookseller of Florence,* Ross King describes "the inadvertent eye-skip" that would plague medieval scribes as they unwittingly dropped a word—or even a line—while hand-copying a work.

Can you guess at least one of these two words?

    **a. pareidolia**    **b. cloud-cuckoo-land**    **c. parablepsis**

**Answers:** Number 1 is **c: mollify.** Number 2 is **b: skeuomorph.** Number 3 is **a: pareidolia,** for the first word, and **c: parablepsis,** for the second.

**Inkhorn answers:** These words do not appear in the online *Merriam-Webster:* aberuncate, allubescency, excubation, gemelliparous, salsamentarious. All the others in the list do. Should we start an Adopt-an-Inkhorn movement?

## 12.
## NO ACADEMY, PLEASE: IT'S ENGLISH

You're having a dinner party to which you've invited William Shakespeare, Samuel Johnson, and Jonathan Swift. You're wondering how the conversation will go and hoping that no one will want seconds.

The ever-voluble Shakespeare will never be at a loss for words, because if the right word is lurking somewhere in the English lexicon, he's likely to know it. And if it isn't, he's apt to invent one. That will cause Johnson to surcease from his customary scowl and instruct the amanuensis he brought along to capture words that Shakespeare is summoning; he's to do so by writing them onto small slips of paper. Later, Johnson will feed these words into the maw of his giant dictionary that he's been laboring over for years. He might even share some with his heavyweight literary circle, one of whose members is William Jones of PIE fame.

Swift is the one you want to seat far from the crystal. He's apt to throw down his cutlery and pronounce that this rogue of a language called English should stop its infernal changing! To which Shakespeare might coolly ask just what the *dickens* (one of the words in Will's voluminous vocabulary) he's talking about.

Pass the port. It's going to be a lively evening.

Swift was not the first (or last) of the English-language prescriptivists. Daniel Defoe (1660–1731), of *Robinson Crusoe* fame, preceded him. What English lacked, he and other purists lamented, was an academy to serve as gatekeeper of the language. After all, France had its Académie Française, Spain its Real Academia Española, and Italy its Accademia della Crusca. *Crusca* means bran. "They called themselves that," Ross King tells us, "because they separated the *farina* from the *crusca*—or, as we would say, the wheat from the chaff."

English had neither wheat nor chaff. English had **bupkes** (which is a shortened Yiddish word whose long form means "goat droppings"—in case there's a lull in the conversation at your next dinner party).

**SWIFT: THE FIXER**
Jonathan Swift (1667–1745) undertook his cri de coeur in 1712, sparing few lofty users of the English language from his invective. He vigorously called out the culprits: "illiterate Court-Fops, half-witted Poets, and University Boys." The poets, for example, had the temerity to trim words into contractions to fit a line.

This from a writer who at times went by Isaac Bickerstaff, a name that he simply made up. And who, in the ensuing years, would pen a fantastical tale called *Gulliver's Travels* that embedded two wild and crazy words into the English lexicon: *Lilliputian* and *Brobdingnagian*.

But back to those Court-Fops and Poets.

Swift devoted nearly fifty pages to *A Proposal for Correcting, Improving and Ascertaining the English Tongue.* His solution: that academy again. It was the only way to stop what Swift saw as the "corruption" of English.

"The important thing," Jack Lynch tells us in his book *The Lexicographer's Dilemma*, "was to stop the perpetual change, even if it meant fixing the language before it had achieved perfection."

# Don't fence me in

Swift and Defoe were hardly eccentrics in this endeavor; many other Englishmen piled on. The idea even sailed across the Pond, where some of those one-time English, now Americans, took up the cause. John Adams—an unflinching champion of independence and the revolution it took to get it—thought an academy with its various restrictions would be a great idea. The new democracy, however, thought otherwise.

And so English continues to play true to the trope that its only constancy is change. The only thing unbudgeable about English is its stubborn refusal to not move. That makes it ripe for bringing in the influence of other languages such as French, Italian, Spanish—and academies be damned. As the historian Cecelia Watson remarks in her book *Semicolon,* "rules will be, just as they always have been, inadequate to form a protective fence around English."

**JOHNSON: THE CONVERT**
Samuel Johnson (1709–1784) realized this the hard way. When he set out in 1747 to write his immense dictionary of the English language (two Brobdingnagian volumes, 2,300 pages, and 42,773 entries), he made clear his intent that the "purity" of the English language would "be preserved."

But by the time he published his magnificent tome in 1755, Johnson had realized that English was a tumultuous tongue that would not be tamed. You could not, in his word, "embalm" it. And he was now okay with that. His epiphany probably contributed to the facetious definition he gave his own profession of lexicographer in the *Dictionary*: "A writer of dictionaries; a harmless drudge." In his Preface, Johnson even took a swipe at Swift and "his petty treatise on the *English* language."

Lynch says that for Johnson, "the whole idea of being a literary dictator had come to seem naïve at best and offensive at worst. What's more, it was futile."

While Johnson did not become a lexemic autocrat, his *Dictionary* did become the defining work of the English language for more than a century. One result of this, more by default than design, was that the *Dictionary* did come to "fix" one aspect of English: a fair amount of its spelling. When you're the biggest and most authoritative game in town, you can do that. (At least until Noah Webster comes along.)

# The dictionary of a revolution

Johnson's was not the first dictionary of the English language. Robert Cawdrey, for instance, came out with his "table alphabeticall of hard usual English wordes" in 1604. It was the first monolingual dictionary for English speakers. But most definitions were limited to a few words ("dissimulation" was defined as "dissembly"), etymologies were confined to an occasional "[fr]" for French and "[gr]" for German, and he tended to favor nouns and adjectives.

Johnson went further on his etymologies (although later lexicographers would disprove some of them). He often brought in the Latin, Dutch, German, Italian, or French word the English equivalent derived from; or pointed out if, like "kern," the term was "an Irish word." And he presented Greek and Saxon (Old English) origins in their alphabets. The many ingredients that went into the bouillabaisse called English were unmistakable.

Not that he always approved of a word that English had corralled. The French *finesse*, Johnson pronounced, was "an unnecessary word, creeping into the language." Nevertheless, he let it crawl right into his *Dictionary*, because it was a word that people were using. This utility was a defining characteristic of Johnson's work, and an idea that was quite revolutionary in its day.

Speaking of revolutionary—ironically, this Englishman's dictionary was the one that Thomas Jefferson and other framers of America's Declaration of Independence from England would turn to. But Johnson angrily called out the larger irony: namely, how a country that enslaved people was fighting for its freedom.

## 'Friends, Romans, countrymen, lend me your verse'

What really distinguished Johnson's *Dictionary* were the thousands of entries that featured the work of a leading writer to show the word in use. Not surprisingly, Shakespeare was the most frequently quoted.

"Dissemble," for example, first gets a definition, albeit still brief ("to play the hypocrite"). But Johnson believed that the way to grasp the true sense of a word was to read how an esteemed writer used it. So for "dissemble," he included this sample passage from Shakespeare's *Richard III*: "I am curtail'd of this fair proportion,/Cheated of feature by dissembling nature,/Deform'd, unfinish'd."

The passage is one of four. And while Johnson reached most often for Big Will, his big dictionary is a veritable repository for those he considered the great writers of the English language. Among them: Milton, Francis Bacon, Walter Raleigh, John Dunne, Isaac Newton, Edmund Spenser—and yes, Daniel Defoe and Jonathan Swift.

**SHAKESPEARE: THE SHOWRUNNER**
It's droll: the writer Johnson quoted most in his *Dictionary*, William Shakespeare (1564–1616), had no practical dictionary to refer to. Instead, the Bard of the Celtic-named Avon pretty much *became* one. Shakespeare did the language—and the lexicographers—a huge favor by committing words to both paper and dramatic presentation.

Shakespeare is usually credited for playing a role in seventeen hundred words. To say he invented all of them is likely a stretch. Better to say that he was an innovator and immortalizer of the language, making a slew of words more familiar to more people. As Crystal *père et fils* observe in *The Shakespeare Miscellany*, "Shakespeare's enormously creative linguistic power resides not in the number of words he knew, but in how he used them."

And how, as a result, we still use them. Think **salad days** and **wild goose chase, strange bedfellows** and **green-eyed monsters.** Shakespeare turned verbs into nouns—**embrace, bump**—and nouns into verbs—**cake, cow.** Just the kind of acrobatics that an academy might make much ado about.

Far better to make much ado about the facility with which we can enliven the ever-elastic English language, especially when it's in the hands of a master word geek like Will. It's why **caters** lands a role in *As You Like It,* **enmesh** in *Othello,* **go-between** in *The Merry Wives of Windsor,* and **scuffle** (as a noun) in *Antony and Cleopatra.* As for *Hamlet,* what could be more fitting than **ranting.** The showrunner is in full command of the language, coaxing more words to the fore with performances that linger long in memory.

And as some modern-day research is demonstrating, Shakespeare's manipulative mastery of English seems to quite literally make an impression on our brains. In 2016 Robert McCrum, one of *The Story of English* authors, described the neurological work that Professor Philip Davis of Liverpool University in England had undertaken about ten years earlier in the name of the Bard. Davis was using fMRI scans to see what kind of neurological responses Shakespeare's language elicited when the study's volunteers read him. As McCrum reported, "It is Shakespeare's inventions—particularly his deliberate syntactic errors like changing the part of speech of an individual word—that really excite us."

Welcome to your brain on Shakespeare.

―――〜〜〜―――

Back to that dinner party.

As your guests take their leave, Shakespeare hangs back and pulls you aside with a request. Next time, might you include some new blood—say, from the twenty-first century? He suggests some of those irrepressible American cousins, whom he feels a special affinity for. As Stephen Greenblatt, the Pulitzer Prize-winning scholar and author of the biography *Will in the World*, observes: "Shakespeare shares with the English language itself—his language—a remarkable openness to linguistic innovation by immigrant cultures. In that sense, Shakespeare is the quintessentially American author."

You make a note to invite two American writers the next time. The first is Reid Byers, the author of *The Private Library*, who decided we needed a word to describe the quiet euphoria of being in a room where books reign.

"I searched for a long time for the right word," he confesses in an online Q&A with his publisher, Oak Knoll Press. "*Imbooked, beshelved, inlibriated, circumvolumed,* and *peribibliated* were candidates, but they didn't quite cut it." Then he found it: **book-wrapt.** "It implies the traditional library wrapped in shelves of books, and the condition of rapt attention to a particular volume," he explains.

The second invitation will go to the author John Koenig, who has become quite the word coiner. In *The Dictionary of Obscure Sorrows,* Koenig has created words we thought we had no words for—like **looseleft,** which he defines as "feeling a sense of loss upon finishing a good book."

Not surprisingly, many of Koenig's neologisms are flavored with the English language's secret sauce: their origins lie in French, Greek, Latin, Spanish, German, Italian, and—thank you, America—Lakota.

## Words in Shakespeare with Some Wondrous Origins

Match the word on the left with the term on the right that suggests its origin.

(Don't peek—the answers follow.)

|     |              |              |
| --- | ------------ | ------------ |
| 1.  | auspicious   | a. woods     |
| 2.  | generous     | b. to bite   |
| 3.  | remorseless  | c. reminder  |
| 4.  | savagery     | d. birth     |
| 5.  | to humor     | e. birds     |
| 6.  | deracinate   | f. bribery   |
| 7.  | embrace      | g. moisture  |
| 8.  | monumental   | h. radish    |
| 9.  | to elbow     | i. pimp      |
| 10. | pander       | j. bagel     |

**1. auspicious: birds**
Start with the Latin *auspex*, then go further back to PIE's *\*awi-spek*, and there you have it: an observer of birds. *Spek* becomes the Latin *specere* (look at); *awi* becomes *avis* (bird). But what, you may reasonably wonder, does a birdwatcher have to do with a word that means "opportune" or "fortunate"?

The Romans believed that the behavior of birds held portents for the future that an auspex, or birdwatcher, could explain. The auspex was in effect a soothsayer.

The idea is not that far-fetched. Birds are known to be fairly good weather forecasters, at least when an *in*auspicious storm is brewing and their flight patterns change. In fact, an ornithologist has found at least one species of bird to be a reliable predictor of the annual hurricane season, months before any storm starts brewing.

## 2. generous: birth

*Gene* is a PIE root that means to beget or give birth. You'll also find it rooting around in other English words, including "congenial," "engender," "genuine," "indigenous," and "primogeniture." The Sanskrit *janati* means to beget; the Welsh *geni* is to be born.

The French and Latin versions of "generous" indicated "of noble birth." This eventually came to mean a nobility of spirit, which is how English uses the word, and you don't have to be a nobleman or noblewoman to be generous.

## 3. remorseless: to bite

This has its roots in the Latin *mordere,* "to bite"; the *re* indicates "to bite back." *Mordere* also gives us "mordant," one definition of which is "biting." In Chaucer's day, you could also express the idea as a verb: *remord. Mord* might have begun as the root *\*mer-* in PIE, meaning "to harm." When we're remorseless, we're merciless. The "biting" is not literal, but it can inflict pain just the same.

## 4. savagery: woods

The ferociousness of "savagery" begins with the suggested serenity of "sylvan." Start with the Latin *silva,* or forest, extend it to *salvatious,* which in Old French becomes *salvage* and *sauvage.* Suddenly that serenity becomes wild and primitive—savage.

What is it about forests and woods, anyway? They also figure into the meaning of *pagan.*

## 5. to humor: moisture

The Latin this springs from, *umor,* is a noun whose meaning includes "body fluid." At one time the leading medicinal theory held that the body contained four humors: blood, phlegm, and two kinds of bile—yellow and black. (Ewww.) The blood and the phlegm were the moist humors. (Double ewww.) These humors determined your frame of mind. At some point, "humor" became attached to the notion of being amusing; as a verb, it indicated a willingness to indulge someone.

It might be best not to carry a picture in your head of this origin if someone asks you to humor them.

### 6. deracinate: radish
The word traces back to the Latin *radix,* meaning "root." *Radix* is also the root of "radish." The idea of de-rooting initially applied only to pulling up plants from the ground. Then this literal meaning acquired a figurative sense of uprooting, or being uprooted. It could be worse: we could be talking about "eradicating"—another word that sprang up from *radix.*

### 7. embrace: bribery
In Middle English, the noun "embrace" was another word for "bribery." But people grasped onto a different meaning of the word: "hug." You hug with your arms, the Greek singular of which is *brakhim.* Latin stuck close to that with *brachium.* The Spanish *los brazos,* or arms, often lead to *los abrazos,* or hugs—which brings us neatly back to embrace.

### 8. monumental: reminder
"Monument" is from the Latin *monumentum,* which derives from *monere,* "to remind." (PIE had the similar \*moneie.) Monuments are indeed reminders—of a grave, for instance, as the Old French *monument* indicated. Now something monumental suggests an event or idea of such significance, we're not apt to forget it.

### 9. **to elbow: bagel**
"Elbow" was a noun well before Shakespeare verbified it. It's a marriage of two PIE roots, *\*el-* and *\*bheng,* the latter meaning "to bend." That second root is also what gives the word **bagel** (from the Yiddish *beygl*) its bend.

### 10. **pander: pimp**
During the fourteenth century, the Italian writer Giovanni Boccaccio would write the epic poem *Il filostrato,* which would inspire the English writer Chaucer to write *his* epic poem, *Troilus and Criseyde,* which would in turn become the basis of Shakespeare's play, *Troilus and Cressida.* (Patience: the pander part is coming.) The character Pandarus in all these works is the one who hooks up the two for an affair of the heart and then some. Thus "pander" often carries a disapproving tone of catering to vulgarity.

# 13.
# THE EMPIRE STRIKES

In the December 2022/January 2023 issue of *Wired* Magazine, the article titled "The Hibernator's Guide to the Galaxy" carried this provocative lead-in:

> Scientists are on the verge of figuring out how to put humans in a state of suspended animation. It could be the key to colonizing Mars.

*Colonizing?*
Better pack light for Mars: "colonizing" is a word that carries a lot of baggage.

## Corporatizing colonizing

"Colonizer" starts off bland enough in the *Oxford English Dictionary* as "one who colonizes" (1781). An interesting side dish of the word crops up in 1808, when Sir Walter Rauley is described as "that great coloniarch." (If you're having a who-he? moment over "Rauley," it's "Raleigh" to us now; in the day, it was another instance of that fluid English spelling.) But by 1957, this quotation in the *OED* entry, from a weekly magazine in Britain called *Listener,* reflects a markedly different perspective:

> "Colonialism" is the commonest term of abuse nowadays throughout more than half the world.

As late as 1940, the historian Daniel Immerwahr tells us, almost a third of the world's population had been colonized.

Rewind to the 1600s, when the British established the East India Company. Despite being headquartered in just one London office complex with fewer than three dozen employees, the East India Company became a powerful international trading conglomerate that made the Viking invade-and-trade model look like a neighborhood swap meet. The EIC *ruled*—quite literally, as it paved the way for British rule of India until 1947.

"Almost single-handedly," William Dalrymple tells us in *The Anarchy*, the EIC's takeover of India's Mughal Empire in the mid-1700s "reversed the balance of trade, which from Roman times on had led to a continued drain of Western bullion eastwards." What in India was a *mughal* in English became a **mogul**.

## Island swap

Britain's presence in India was, indeed, lengthy. But the East India Company was just one of what Theodore Roosevelt described in his 1891 history of his hometown of New York as "commercial corporations of imperial power." The Dutch West India Company, comparably chartered, was up and running in 1621.

Shortly after that, the Dutch company claimed ownership of what Roosevelt described as "a mass of tangled, frowning forest, fringed with melancholy marshes." That would be the island of Manhattan—or New Amsterdam, as the Dutch named it. The name barely had time to sink into those melancholy marshes before Britain, at war with the Netherlands, claimed the island in 1664.

The Dutch shrugged off the loss because they held onto something they considered more valuable under the terms of the peace treaty: the Banda Islands in Indonesia, including one that the British had controlled. It gained the Dutch a monopoly on a major source of the spice that Europeans were endowing with near-magical powers—it was an aphrodisiac, a hallucinogen, a protection against the plague.

The island of Manhattan was swapped for the islands of nutmeg.

Corporate colonizing was not the ambit of just the British and the Dutch. Even Sweden had a go of it, establishing in 1638 a New Sweden in the area around what is today Wilmington, Delaware. If you missed that chapter in American history, it's because you blinked. Within two decades, the Dutch had taken over the settlement.

## 'A fourth part'

The Dutch were not the first Europeans to lay claim to many of the Banda Islands. They were just the ones who muscled out Portugal. But as valuable as the Banda Islands, and India, and other parts of Asia as well as Africa became to the Europeans, the attraction to what they called the "New World" was astronomical—in the sense of huge. And we can make an astronomical comparison here—this "astronomical" in the sense that space scientists use it.

We earthlings know that the Earth's moon is in what's called outer space. But there's a realm beyond outer space, called deep space.

The Europeans of the sixteenth and seventeenth centuries hadn't gotten to compartmentalizing the heavens yet. But they did have their own way of compartmentalizing the Earth. Here's how Isidore, a seventh-century scholar and archbishop of Seville, laid it out:

> It is divided into three parts, one of which is called Asia, the second Europe, the third Africa . . . . Apart from these three parts of the world there exists a fourth part, beyond the ocean, which is unknown to us.

Toby Lester presents Isidore's words as the epigraph of his book, aptly titled *The Fourth Part of the World*. Those three parts were like outer space and the fourth part, like deep space. And "fourth part," as Lester tells us, was still shorthand for the Americas into the sixteenth century. Many Europeans were as keen then to gain a foothold in this fourth part as many space lovers are now to get to Mars. And to colonize it.

## Why Spanish and French beat out Portuguese

Thus Portugal and Spain drew an audacious line in the sand—actually, on a map—in the 1494 Treaty of Tordesillas. The treaty assigned the rule of "New World" lands from most of Brazil eastward to Portugal, and those lands westward to Spain. The mind boggles.

By 1603, France's Samuel de Champlain was in New France—what became Canada—and had founded Quebec within five years. In the coming decades, France would hold large swaths of eastern Canada as well as that land to the south, from the Acadia region that included eastern Maine, to the Great Lakes and Upper Midwest, to New Orleans in Louisiana.

England also planted its flag in parts of Canada, founding the Hudson's Bay Company in 1670 and setting up trading posts to ply the profitable fur trade.

France, Spain, England, and the Netherlands further claimed islands in the **Caribbean.** They would have considered the islands the West Indies, a holdover from Columbus's certainty that he had reached India. *Caribbean* derives from the name of some of the Native inhabitants, the Caribs.

It goes without saying that none of the Indigenous people in this fourth part were consulted in any meaningful way in all of this colonizing.

Ironically, one of the European groups that eventually came to America was not intent on colonizing but rather, simply settling. That was the Germans—the very group whose ancestors had been the ones to invade the island of Britain back in the day and start this thing called English.

## Staying the unsteady course

In the midst of all this uprooting and upheaval, the English language maintained its usual course: shifting and morphing. In the US, where we're going to land for the rest of this book, there was a French that often sounded worlds away from Paris, and a Spanish that became markedly different from the language spoken in much of Spain.

Other languages left their echoes in place-names. The Dutch, for starters, on that vexed marshy island. To them we owe what we call

*Brooklyn, Harlem*, and the farms where, as Roosevelt described them in his history of New York, "the settlers raised wheat, rye, buckwheat, flax, and beans, while their herds and flocks throve apace." Those farms—in Dutch, *bouwerij*—became one of Manhattan's oldest, and sometimes infamous, streets: the *Bowery*. The stairs, or *stoeps*, that the Dutch built to put a bit of distance between the streets and the houses they built became the **stoops** where some New Yorkers still park themselves on warm days. And, as the language mapper Josh Katz graphically demonstrates in *Speaking American*, they are where you may not find yard sales or garage sales, but you just might find signs for stoop sales. (Not yet spotted: bumper stickers announcing "I stoop for stoop sales.")

Britain's words of empire—most notably, from India—slid right into English, as we shall see in the "Screen Stars" vignette. Eventually, though, British English would take on a different sound once it sailed west from that fair scepter'd isle to that newer England. And the languages of America's Indigenous peoples would be among those to enrich American English in countless ways.

Oh, and did we mention New Spain? Time to head across the Pond. As for Mars—maybe just pay a visit.

## Of Turnips and Toppled Trees

With the exception of *smorgasbord*, few words beyond the Viking era that are exclusively Swedish have entered English (no, ABBA and Ikea don't count). There is this one, though, which you're more likely to hear in England than the US: **swede**.

No, really: "swede," and even "Swede," is what we're talking when we're talking turnip types. And these types are likely to turn up in those Cornish pasties we encountered in chapter 3. The root vegetable that the English call swede/Swede is what Americans call **rutabaga.** That word is, shall we say, rooted in the Swedish *rotabagge*. The *rot* means "root," and the rest of the word indicates a small sack.

The first small wave of Swedes who arrived during that short-lived New Sweden left something other than words that settled into the American lexicon. It was a particular kind of dwelling they built that would become part of American lore and be forever grafted onto the story of Abraham Lincoln: the log cabin. The wooden structures that the Swedes fashioned from felled trees were not intended to be permanent. No matter—they permanently reside in the vernacular of the American frontier. The National Park Service describes log cabins as "enmeshed in American history, folklore, and myth."

And while there would never be another Swedish colony in America, there would be more than a million Swedes who would later immigrate in the late 1800s and early 1900s. In his book *The Viking Heart: How Scandinavians Conquered the World,* the historian Arthur Herman shares how one new arrival to America summed up the hope of the immigrant: "to love the old country like a mother and love the new country like a bride." Doesn't that just conquer your heart?

## Screen Stars

Like the curries that India is famous for, many of the words from this country that entered English really know how to spice up a sentence. Maybe that's why a number of them make their way into movie titles, both in Bollywood and Hollywood. Here are seven, with some backstories on the words. As for the films themselves, we'll leave the reviews to the **pundits**—another Hindi and Sanskrit word the Brits picked up, meaning wise or learned.

*Gimme the* **Loot***.* You might say that both Hindi and Sanskrit words were plundered in the shaping of this word. "Loot" means just that—plunder—when it's a verb. Use it as a noun and it becomes the spoils that you've just plundered.

*Avatar.* The Sanskrit root means "descent," as in the way a god drops down to earth and is incarnated as a human. We could use "embodiment" or "epitome" in roughly the same way as "avatar," but the movie moguls must have figured that those words didn't sound like the stuff of sky-high box-office grosses.

***Brahman** Naman.* In the Hindu caste system, you can't get any higher than Brahman. And very few do—mainly priests; the word suggests prayer. Ironically, in equal-opportunity America, a New England version of this caste evolved: the Boston Brahmin. Unless you were among the first Europeans to hop off the boats from England, you didn't have a prayer of becoming one of these rich, educated elites. Oliver Wendell Holmes, a poet who was also dean of Harvard's medical school, anointed this bunch with the title in the nineteenth century. He knew them well: he was one such Boston Brahmin.

***Juggernaut.*** The story goes that the Hindu god Vishnu, aka "lord of the world," aka *Jagannath,* would ride through the streets in a ginormous carriage. This behemoth of a buggy had a propensity for crushing the pious who threw themselves in its path. English's propensity is to assign an abstract quality to this bruiser: a force relentless and resistant to being stopped in its tracks. Some would suggest that "juggernaut" describes the English language.

*The Man in the **Seersucker** Suit.* It's a toss-up as to which is the more comical—that this truly is the name of a movie or what the source of the word turns out to be. "Seer!" someone shouts, way in the back of the theater. Nope. "Sucker!" from someone else in the cheap seats. No again. But you already knew it couldn't be that simple. Hindi, Urdu, and Persian all thread through this fabric's linguistic lineage. The charm of seersucker is how the striped fabric alternates between smooth and crinkly. Rather like the texture of (wait for it) . . . milk and sugar.

*The **Pajama** Game.* Or, if you want to be British about it, ***Pyjama** Girls.* It's the very same word in Hindi, *pajama,* and means almost the very same thing: loose-fitting trousers that are lightweight.

*The Last **Nabobs**.* The late political speechwriter William Safire, an avatar of alliteration, achieved word-nerd nirvana with his "nattering nabobs of negativism." It dates to 1970 and a speech Safire wrote for Richard Nixon's vice president, Spiro Agnew. Nixon and Agnew had plenty of opponents, and this was the dismissive phrase for the naysayers that Safire crafted. "Nabob" signifies a wealthy and influential person. Juxtaposed with "nattering," though, the status deflates from important to self-important. But a shortened version of "nabob" assumes its lofty heights as the name of the iconic street in San Francisco: Nob Hill. It was once home to nineteenth-century railroad barons and their over-the-top mansions.

## That's How the CAPTCHA Crumbles

Pretend this is one of those CAPTCHA quizzes where you must determine which element in the frame is the odd one out. Guessing correctly indicates you're human. Or possibly AI.

So . . . which of these four Dutch words doesn't belong with the rest?

*koekje*
*krullen*
*wafel*
*snoepen*

Here they are in English:

cookie
cruller (from the Dutch for "curl")
waffle
snoop

Seems like a no-brainer, doesn't it? "Snoop" has to be the interloper.

Now for the *gotcha:*

*Snoepen* is this delightful Dutch verb that describes sneaking some sweets in secret. So all four words are connected.

But in case you think that snoop is a stretch—that it is, in fact, a bunch of B.S.—assume your upper-crustiest pose and pronounce it to be **poppycock.** You'll be channeling the Dutch word *pappekak,* meaning soft dung.

# PART TWO:
# THE POND, WEST

"... For English is a language that simply cannot be fixed, nor can its use ever be absolutely laid down. It changes constantly; it grows with an almost exponential joy. It evolves eternally; its words alter their senses and their meanings subtly, slowly, or speedily according to fashion and need."

—Simon Winchester,
*The Meaning of Everything:*
*The Story of the Oxford English Dictionary*

# 14.
## *MABRÍKA* TO AMERICA

Within the Library of Congress's vast collections in Washington, DC, a book of particular historical import is considered so significant, it's been said that when it moves within the Library, an armed escort moves along with it.

Few outside the Library have seen the book, and not many more know it exists. At a viewing a number of years ago, a small group stood on all sides of a long, rectangular table in a windowless room within the Library. Their talk was subdued, their faces thoughtful, their hands occasionally gesturing. Nobody touched the book that was the object of their attention.

The book dates from 1502, but its history dates to 1492 and the arrival of three ships, sailing under the Spanish flag, finally making landfall in what Europeans liked to call the New World.

The book is Christopher Columbus's *Book of Privileges,* with sheet after sheet of vellum lettered in line after line of precise calligraphy. Here are the royal charters and other legal documents that constitute Columbus's business deal with Spain's king and queen. Here are all the details of how they would run these new lands, which had somehow become their lands.

Chet van Duzer is one of three scholars who parsed the *Privileges* in essays for a 2014 facsimile publication. Here is one of the portions he extracted, in which Columbus underscores the consequence of his landing:

> ... *por voluntad divina, he puesto so el señorío del Rey e de la Reyna, nuestros señores, otro mundo, y por donde la España, que hera dicha pobre, es la más rica.*

> ... by divine will, I have put another world under the sovereignty of the king and queen, our lords, and consequently, Spain, once considered poor, is now the richest.

There were, of course, myriad other consequences, particularly for the Indigenous peoples who had been living in this fourth part of the world. For them, this was no New World. It was *their* world, soon to be irrevocably changed as wave after wave of Europeans arrived, century after century.

*Mabríka* to America.

## The first encounter of two worlds

***Mabríka*** means "welcome" in the Taíno language. "Scholars believe that the Taíno originally migrated from Venezuela to the Caribbean and across the Antilles as early as 400 B.C.," writes John Hessler, the former curator of the Library's Jay I. Kislak Collection of the Archaeology & History of the Early Americas, in an essay for the facsimile publication.

It wasn't just their longevity that set them apart in modern history. The Taíno, says Hessler, "were the first New World peoples that Columbus and his crews encountered." Two years later, Columbus would enlist a Spanish friar, Ramon Pané, to accompany him on his second expedition to the Americas and to live among the Taíno. Pané was to learn the customs and languages of this Arawak Indian group.

While we may never know what words were exchanged during that first encounter, we do know that certain Taíno words became Spanish words, and a number of those became English words. The same would happen with Aztec, or Nahuatl, in what became Mexico, and Inca, or Quechua, in the Andes. As Cody Cassidy observed in his book, *Who*

*Ate the First Oyster?*, "when cultures adopt foreign [Cassidy's word—he hasn't gotten the memo] technology they typically adopt the originating culture's terminology as well." As the Spanish did with *barbacoa,* or **barbecue**, for example.

A comparable borrowing occurred with other Indigenous languages, notably with place-names, when the Spanish and French and English headed for more northerly destinations, like *Arizona* and *Wisconsin* and *Massachusetts.*

## All dead? DNA begs to differ

But what became of the people involved in that initial face-to-face? Less than fifty years after that first meeting in 1492, the nearly three million Taíno had all but disappeared. The official story was that the Taíno had been erased.

"Around the 1600s, the Spanish governors of the islands basically wrote back to the Crown and said, 'The Taíno are all gone, they're dead, they're exterminated,'" relays Priscilla Colón.

Except, says Colón, that they weren't. And she is among those who have the DNA testing to prove it—a reminder that in history, it's not just the telling but who's telling it. In fact, the geneticist Martínez Cruzado estimates that today, 61 percent of Puerto Ricans have Taíno in their blood.

Colón, a Spanish/English American bilingual, is a longtime translator and educational curriculum developer who cofounded Casa Areyto, an initiative to reclaim the Taíno language and culture. She traces her ancestry to Borikén, the Taíno name for Puerto Rico, where her parents were born, and where the Taíno had a strong cultural and linguistic foothold. Borikén was home to numerous Taíno chiefdoms, possibly as many as twenty.

## Awakening a sleeping language

While it was not true that all the Taíno had died off in the 1600s, it is true that there are no longer any living speakers of the original Taíno language. Which is why, as Colón says, "it's known as a sleeping language."

She is among the cohort of language professionals creating a modern version of it. The original was never a recorded language, leaving it even more vulnerable. The recreation is written as well as oral. And Casa Areyto's educational materials are in both English and Spanish.

## When additions mean a loss in translation

As Cassidy pointed out, when a culture encounters something they have no word for, they'll often adapt the native word. But as Colón points out, they don't always get it right.

One of the Spanish words for a chief is *el cacique*. It comes from the Taíno *kasíke*. Seems straightforward enough: just a different spelling, which is common.

Except that, in Taíno, there is no gender distinction for the word like the masculine *el* in Spanish. Filtering the word through the prism of the borrowing language added something that wasn't there.

"*Kasíke* was originally a gender-neutral term that could refer to male and female," Colón explains. And, she adds, there were female chiefs among the Taíno before the arrival of the Spanish.

The psycholinguist Viorica Marian, citing recent experiments in brain cognition, shows how strongly a gendered word can affect its perception. Speakers of German, she says, often describe a bridge as "elegant," "fragile," and "peaceful." Speakers of Spanish are more apt to portray it as "big," "sturdy," and "towering." Guess which language has a feminine modifier for "bridge," and which a masculine?

## Discovering a new world of language

The story of the Taíno's encounter with European empire is one that played out with all the Indigenous peoples throughout the Americas in the centuries to come. Each had its own specific tragedies. Much was lost, but there remains much resilience.

Just one example is in the Spanish that many Puerto Ricans, Cubans, and Dominicans speak today. Colón says that her native-Spanish-speaking friends who are not from the Caribbean will tease her about some of the words she uses, terms they've never heard. One of them is *jurutungo*. "It's a word that only Puerto Ricans use to mean very, very far away," says Colón. Now she understands why her friends find it a head-scratcher. "That's the Taíno talking."

## Who Saw the First *Squuncke*?

*Never mind who ate the first oyster,* the early English settlers to Massachusetts and points south might have said, *what are those four-legged creatures we're seeing for the first time*? Native Americans knew exactly what they were, so their terms became the basis of the English words.

Bet you can guess all of these. Keep in mind that the spellings are just one phonetic version of the Algonquian:

> apousoum
> arahkun
> atchitamon
> moos
> musquash
> squuncke

Okay, if you really feel you need them—here are the answers, but with their order scrambled: **chipmunk, muskrat, moose, possum, skunk, raccoon.**

# Like Water for *Xocoatl*

As French was with Latin, so Spanish was with several Indigenous languages—the water carrier by which new words seeped into the language. Then English promptly soaked up the Spanish. Watch how these three languages flow—one from the Caribbean (Taíno), one from Mesoamerica (Nahuatl, the language of the Aztecs), and one from South America (Quechua, the language of the Inca).

| Taíno/Arawak | Spanish | English |
| --- | --- | --- |
| barbakóa | barbacoa | barbecue |
| batáta | patata | potato |
| hamáka | hamaca | hammock |
| hurakán | huracán | hurricane |
| káiku | cayo | cay |
| kanóa | canoa | canoe |
| mahís | maíz | maize |
| sabána | sabana | savannah |

**BITE-SIZE SIDELIGHTS:**
- The Cayman Islands got their name from the Taíno *kaimán,* which means crocodile.
- This might just blow you away about that *hurakán:* as Cynthia Barnett tells us, today's satellite imagery of a hurricane bears an uncanny resemblance to the depiction of it on Taíno pottery.

## e pluribus ENGLISH

| Nahuatl (Aztec/Mexica) | Spanish | English |
|---|---|---|
| āhuacatl | aguacate | avocado |
| cacahuatl | cacao | cocoa |
| chilli | chile | chili pepper |
| coyōtl | coyote | coyote |
| ocelotl | ocelote | ocelot |
| tomatl | tomate | tomato |
| xocoatl | chocolate | chocolate |

**BITE-SIZE SIDELIGHTS:**
- Fittingly, the word **guacamole**—*ahuacamulli* in Nahuatl—echoes its creation: it's a mix of that āhuacatl (avocado) and *mōlli*, meaning sauce (*mole* in Spanish).
- The Aztecs would have known *coyōtl* as the four-legged animal. More recently, undocumented immigrants who tried to come from Mexico to the US knew the coyote to be the human smugglers some relied on, provided they could pay the exorbitant fee these coyotes demanded.

| Quechua | Spanish | English |
|---|---|---|
| cuntur | cóndor | condor |
| ch'arki | charqui | jerky |
| kina | quina | quinine |
| kinua | quinoa | quinoa |
| wik'uña | vicuña | vicuna |
| yapa | la ñapa | lagniappe |

**BITE-SIZE SIDELIGHTS:**
- *Machu Picchu* is Quechua for old (*machu*) mountain peak (*picchu* or *pikchu*). That sounds about right for that lofty Incan city in Cusco, Peru. But the name of that dizzyingly high peak directly behind the ancient city in the clouds is Huayna Picchu, or young mountain. There's newfound evidence dating back to the sixteenth century that Huayna Picchu is the way the locals referred to the entire area.
- Look—you're trilingual! The Quechua word **puma**, another term for cougar, is the same word in Spanish and English. So is **llama**.

## Is Your State Name a Native American Name?

Here are a few clues:

**Not if it's named after a personage.** That means neither of the Carolinas (the Latin for Charles, as in the English king) or Delaware (Lord De La Warr, in case that sailed right past you in American history). It also knocks out Georgia, Louisiana, Maryland, Pennsylvania, both Virginias, and Washington.

**Not if it's an echo of a place from across the Pond.** That takes New Hampshire, New Jersey, and New York out of the running.

**Not if it's Spanish.** *Adiós,* California, Colorado, Florida, Montana, Nevada, and New Mexico. Actually, New Mexico could go either way, as *Mexico* is Nahuatl.

**Not if it's one of these three New England states: Rhode Island, Vermont, or Maine.** *Roode Eylandt,* meaning Red Island, is what the Dutch navigator Adrian Block christened Rhode Island. Apparently, he spotted red clay from his ship. Vermont owes its name to the French explorer Samuel de Champlain: *Verd* (or *Vert*) *Mont*, meaning Green Mountain. As for Maine, pick from several theories, starting with King Charles's 1639 charter naming it Mayne.

**Not if it's Indiana or Idaho.** Indiana is named *for* Native Americans ("land of the Indians") but not *from* a Native American term. Neither is Idaho, much as some in the 1860s tried to pass off the fabricated name as Shoshone.

Even so, Native American place-names abound throughout the country. Here's just a handful: *Minquadale* in Delaware; *Hackensack* in New Jersey, meaning "mouth of a river"; *Skalkaho* in Montana; *Kooskia* in Idaho, which appears in journals from the Lewis and Clark expedition; and *Quonochontaug*, a name almost as long as the state it's in: Rhode Island.

Here are the states that owe their names to Native American names:

- Alabama
- Alaska
- Arizona
- Arkansas
- Connecticut
- Dakota, North and South
- Illinois
- Iowa
- Kansas
- Kentucky
- Massachusetts
- Michigan
- Minnesota
- Mississippi
- Missouri
- Nebraska
- Ohio
- Oklahoma
- Oregon
- Tennessee
- Texas
- Utah
- Wisconsin
- Wyoming

These are, of course, the English-language versions of the place-names. With Arizona, the English followed the Spanish version of the Native name, and with Wisconsin, the French.

Many of the original names capture a key feature of an area's topography. Thus, Massachusetts is roughly "great hill" and Connecticut "long river," both Algonquian names. Mississippi is Ojibwe for "big river," while Nebraska is Omaha-Ponca and Otoe for "flat river."

Michigan is Potawatomi and Ojibwe for "great lake." Tennessee is named after its eponymous river and is a Cherokee word.

And never will you find the name of an individual, no matter how lofty.

"Indians have viewed such commemorative names as inappropriate: humans are too small, too fleeting and insignificant to have places named for them," writes Doug Herman, a former senior geographer at the Smithsonian's National Museum of the American Indian. "The land is eternal; it owns us, we do not own it."

And how about Hawai'i? The name is from the islands' Native Hawaiian language, which is Polynesian and part of the Austronesian family. England's Captain Cook had a brief go of naming the archipelago in 1778, and aren't we glad it didn't stick: the Sandwich Islands.

## A Written Indigenous Language That Uses No Alphabet

In 1643, Roger Williams, the English settler who established Rhode Island, wrote *A Key into the Language of America, or an Help to the Language of the Natives in That Part of America Called New-England*. He focused on what he called "the Narrogánset Dialect," the language of the region's Narragansett Tribe.

Williams was the first but not the only European American to try to translate Native American languages. But there was one difference: Williams actually practiced what most other Puritans only preached about, religious freedom, so he wasn't trying to convert the Narragansetts to Christianity by speaking to them in their own language. As Ted Widmer, a Rhode Islander and former director of the Library of Congress's John W. Kluge Center, observed, Williams thought "the best way to get at the basic truths of America was to talk with the original Americans themselves."

Which was not what motivated another New Englander named John Eliot, who was all about religious conversion. He published America's first Bible at Harvard College in 1663 in Algonquian, something he was able to do with the help he received from several Indigenous men. There was, however, an unintended consequence beyond conversion efforts, and a happy one. Some three hundred-odd years later, as the Mystic Seaport Museum explained in a related exhibition, the Eliot Bible became a way for Indigenous groups in the area "to relearn and reclaim endangered Algonquian languages."

But while Williams's and Eliot's motives differed, both were efforts of native Indo-European speakers to work with a non-Indo-European language. A member of the Cherokee Nation named Sequoyah changed all that in the 1820s, when he took charge of creating a written version of the language of his people.

Sequoyah devised eighty-five symbols that became the Cherokee syllabary. Unlike an alphabet of letters, or a pictograph of characters, the syllabary contains a distinct sound for each symbol. These syllables are specific to the Cherokee language.

Thanks to the syllabary, within just a few years, most members of the Cherokee Nation were literate in their Native language. Not surprising, then, that the first Native American newspaper was the *Cherokee Phoenix,* written with this syllabary. What might be surprising, given all the languages finding their way to America by the 1820s, is that this was also the country's first bilingual newspaper.

You can see what the syllabary looks like at https://www.americathebilingual.com/talking-leaves-the-cherokee-syllabary-of-sequoyah/.

## The Navajo Code Talkers Were *Ta-eh-ye-sy*

The Battle of Iwo Jima in the spring of 1945 marked a major victory for American troops fighting World War II in the Pacific. What no one but a handful of people knew about until twenty-three years later were some of the Americans who played a key role in it: the Navajo Code Talkers.

"Were it not for the Navajos," according to a high-ranking officer whose statement has appeared on the CIA's public website, "the Marines would never have taken Iwo Jima."

This marked the second war where a Native American language played a critical role: a code developed in the Choctaw language was deployed in World War I. The Navajo language proved ideal for the Second World War because it was so blessedly complex. As the writers of the Marine Corps University website pointed out: "there is no indication that any message traffic in the Navajo language—while undoubtedly intercepted—was ever deciphered."

Approximately 420 Navajo Code Talkers contributed to the war effort, usually from the front lines, and often dodging enemy fire as they set up their bulky radio equipment. As the Allies and the Japanese exchanged fire, the Code Talkers exchanged messages. Their encryption and decryption had to be instant and accurate. "The faster you send the code, the faster you receive, and save somebody's life," explained Bill Toledo, a Navajo Code Talker, in a 2008 retrospective.

The Navajo Marines created the code themselves, a specialized vocabulary separate from what Native speakers would normally use. Even the spelling conventions were different. The men started with more than two hundred words and kept going. "They wouldn't let us carry notes on us while we were studying," Toledo explained. "Everything we had to learn, we had to memorize."

The public first learned of this contribution of the Navajo—or *Diné*, meaning "the people"—in 1968, when the military declassified the information. A peek into the workings of the code gives us a good idea of why no one ever cracked it.

- For starters, the code included certain Navajo terms that stood in for military-related terms. Thus, an eagle—*atsah*—was a transport plane.
- Another aspect of the code tied the twenty-six letters of the English alphabet to Navajo words. The Navajo word for cat, *moasi*, was one of the words that represented the English letter C; *gloe-ih,* or weasel, was W.
- There was a code word for "code": *yil-tas*. Even punctuation had codes: *atsanh* was a rib in Navajo, an apt visualization of a parenthesis. *Tsa-na-dahl* was a tail drop, which in English we call a comma.

## e pluribus ENGLISH

- Other code words were simply translations from English to Navajo. One such was *ta-eh-ye-sy*, meaning vital—exactly what the Navajo Code Talkers were throughout the Allies' war in the Pacific theater.

*It Had to Be Done: The Navajo Code Talkers Remember World War II* contains an appendix of the Navajo Code. Here are just a few of the terms:

| English translation of... | Navajo Code word... | became Navajo code for... |
|---|---|---|
| beaver | *cha* | mine sweeper |
| bird carrier | *tsidi-hey-ye-hi* | aircraft carrier |
| buzzard | *jay-sho* | bomber plane |
| cliff dwelling | *ah-na-sozi* | fortification |
| fish shell | *lo-be-ca* | torpedo |
| humming bird | *da-he-tih-hi* | fighter plane |
| iron fish | *besh-lo* | submarine |
| potatoes | *ni-ma-si* | grenade |
| sand boil | *lesz-yil-beshi* | rocket |
| tortoise | *chay-da-gahi* | tank |

Even though the Navajo Code is no longer a secret, the traditional Navajo language remains elusive to English ears. Paul Zolbrod, a professor of humanities who has studied the language for decades, including during his tenure at Diné College in New Mexico, explained in a phone interview that very few words in Navajo have made their way into English. Zolbrod, who has written on the Navajo creation story and who knew some of the Code Talkers, points out that "there are no regular verbs in Navajo. You learn the language one verb at a time."

Perhaps we could learn two code phrases in a small salute to the Navajo Code Talkers: *na-nil-in* and *ut-zah-ha-dez-bin*, meaning "kept secret, done well."

## Meanderthal Moment: That Humming Sound You Hear Is a Nahuatl God of War

This is one of those Meanderthal tangents that was too good not to wander off into . . .

There is a fierce and tiny bird admired for its frenzy of frenetically flapping wings, which create a sound somewhere between a purr and a growl. "Humming" is an apt description. And so we have, in English, the hummingbird.

Etymologically speaking, how very ho-humm.

The word hardly captures how intrepid these little creatures can be, crossing the tiny sabers of their beaks with another's and dive-bombing interlopers.

Enter the Nahuatl word for them: *huitzilin*.

"In a region that abounded with predatory fauna," observes Jon Dunn in *The Glitter in the Green,* his book on hummingbirds, " . . . it is intriguing that the principal god of war in ancient Mexico should be associated most closely with hummingbirds." Meet the fearsome god Huitzilopochtli, whose name was inspired by the teeny tiny *huitzilin*.

Now, *that's* a humm-dinger of a good word story. And did you notice what term the Navajo Code Talkers assigned to "humming bird"?

## Wampum's True Wealth

Envy the beachcomber on America's Atlantic Coast who comes upon a clam shell revealing a swirl of brilliant purple on its interior. This is the basis for the beads known (in its anglicized form) as wampum. Indigenous Americans hold wampum in high regard—but not as a measure of material wealth.

This despite the fact that some early European Americans did use the beads as money. In fact, the Massachusetts Bay Colony recognized it as currency in 1650. But the idea holds no currency with wampum's creators.

"When beads were collected into strands or woven together as belts, the wampum stood for the authority of a spoken message," explains the Oneida Indian Nation on its website. A treaty, for example, might be finalized with wampum, the pattern of the beads commemorating the historical event.

The more color in the beads, the more weighty the message, which was often memorized. As Cynthia Barnett observes, "the shells were closer to language than coin."

## A Taste of Native Food Names

Here is a bit of backstory on five Indigenous foods in the US whose names English adopted, cooking up its own spellings. See if you can guess the foods.

1. It has many aliases—porgy, sea bream, orata Americana, fair maid, ironsides—and many bones. Its Indigenous name is from the Narragansetts' *mishscuppauog*. But there's still another word for it, inspired by its Native name. Now, if only more seafood lovers would seek out this food. After all, lots of them chowder down on *quahogs* (from another Narragansett word for these large clams), so this name shouldn't be so hard to swallow.
2. The state fruit of North Carolina, it has the Latin name of *Vitis rotundifia*, which nobody uses. One of the state's rivers also bears its name. The river, like the fruit, has an Algonquian name that means "place of the askupo," which is the sweet bay tree.
3. A staple of the Lewis and Clark expedition, this food had been essential long before that for Native American tribes of the North American plains. Its name is from the Cree

language, and its fame was such that European explorers to both poles packed it among their provisions. A mixture of rendered fat and dried meat—often bison—it traveled well in colder climates. Not recommended for low-calorie diets, but there's always keto.

4. It's one of the oldest cultivated crops in North America. The Pueblo tribal nations of New Mexico are among the Indigenous peoples who consider it one of the "three sisters" foods: the essential sources of nutrition. While many Native Americans throughout the US enjoy it, its name originated in the Northeast. It's what the Narragansetts call *askutasquash*.

5. Captain John Smith, he of the Jamestown colony in Virginia, was the first to put the name to paper, in 1629. It is another of these three sisters, although this one undergoes a rather complex culinary process before anyone eats it. The process is called nixtamalization, and knowing its word origin may be all you ever want to know about nixtamalization: it's from Nahuatl. But the name of the "sister" is courtesy of the Powhatan of Virginia: *uskatahomen*.

Did you recognize any of them? They are: (1) the fish also called **scup**, (2) the **scuppernong grape**, (3) **pemmican**, (4) **squash**, and (5) **hominy**, from the "sister" corn. (The third sister is beans.)

# 15.
# SIDE-BY-SIDE-BY-SPANISH

> As the ice in the river was thawing,
> after being frozen for almost four months, . . .
> the departure of Quivira was arranged.
> There, . . . gold and silver would be found.

You've just read a snippet of the account of Spain's Coronado Expedition of 1540–42, as Don Francisco Vázquez de Coronado led a group of Spanish soldiers on yet another of Spain's quests to bring back the most coveted loot of all from the Americas: gold. One of those soldiers, Pedro de Castañeda de Nájera, is the author of this account of their journey, penned a few years after the expedition.

A sprawling, twenty-five-hundred-mile trek, the expedition began in central Mexico and headed north to the land that would adopt the name "America" when it became the United States of it. (The name "America" had actually been there for the taking from at least 1507, when it appeared for the first time on the ginormous world map that the German cartographer Martin Waldseemüller created.)

Quivira was a key destination. It shimmered in the expedition's imagination as "the legendary kingdom of gold," another Oz-like place where those shiny metals that so dazzled the likes of Pizarro and Cortés farther south would be waiting.

Alas, they were not.

As John Miller Morris, professor of political science and geography, dryly observed in his contemporary introduction to de Nájera's narrative, "Unfortunately for the expedition, the boundary between its exploration and its imagination was not sharply defined."

Turns out, Quivira was in Kansas.

## No gold or silver, but silver linings

But never mind. "It was a magnificent contribution to North American geography," Morris explained, "significantly advancing knowledge of the almost unknown Great Plains."

And while there may not have been gold, there was an impressive alloy of cultures in Coronado's entourage. "The *entrada* was notably multicultural as well," according to Morris, using the Spanish term for official incursion, "introducing various ethnic groups to the new lands—Mesoamericans, Afro-Iberians, Spanish, and Portuguese, but also the first French, Italian, German, and English speakers."

Thus, well before Walter Raleigh's long-distance attempt at an English settlement on Roanoke Island off North Carolina's coast in the 1580s, there were significant clusters of Europeans from places other than England, speaking languages other than English, milling about the continental US.

## *Oui* and *sí:* America's first north and south

In the more northerly latitudes of America, it was the French who far outpaced the British in terms of venturing away from the eastern coast.

"The English aristocrats might be building a simulacrum of England in Virginia, . . . and the religious leaders of New England might be building a Shining City on a Hill [Boston]," writes Joel Achenbach in his historical accounting of George Washington's fascination with the West, " . . . but the French were following the fur."

Trappers and merchants, the French were already setting up trading villages in what would become Indiana, Illinois, and Wisconsin by the mid-1600s—not too long after the Puritans were staggering off the *Mayflower* and scuffing their boots on that rock in Plymouth.

## e pluribus ENGLISH

And when Lewis and Clark undertook their legendary expedition west in 1804, they got an assist in translating Native languages not only from Sacagawea, but also from her French-Canadian husband, Toussaint Charbonneau. He was hardly the only native-French speaker in early America who learned an Indigenous language.

In the more southerly latitudes, Spanish traversed America from end to end, essentially bookending the country, with Florida on the east and California on the west.

"The cross following the sword," writes T.D. Allman in *Finding Florida,* "Franciscans and Jesuits eventually established more than one hundred Florida missions, the first of them in 1566, 203 years before the first of the famous California missions was founded."

The oldest European-founded city in America? Florida's St. Augustine—Spain, 1565. The oldest European capital city in America? New Mexico's Santa Fe—Spain again, 1610.

As New Mexico illustrates, in between those bookends were plenty of places that Spain once claimed as part of Mexico, until Mexico broke from Spanish rule in 1821. During that time, much of what we call the American Southwest was like Mexico's northwest. It was with the Treaty of Guadalupe Hidalgo in 1848, which ended the two-year Mexican-American War, that parts of Mexico became part of the US: Arizona, New Mexico, and sections of Utah, Nevada, and Colorado. By then, Texas had already split from Mexico and become part of the US. And by then, Spanish was an established language in all these places.

So although Spanish rule faded into the nineteenth-century tapestry of America, the Spanish language did not. In *An American Language: The History of Spanish in the United States,* the historian Rosina Lozano shows how, even after 1848, many of the government documents in places like New Mexico continued to be written in Spanish. "It serves as a reminder that Spanish is not just an immigrant language in this country, but has very deep roots in the political culture of the nation," she said in an interview.

Those roots radiate beyond the political. "The US and Mexico just rub each other nonstop, 24/7," said Pati Jinich, the Mexican American chef known for her PBS television series *Pati's Mexican Table,* in a podcast interview. "You have the Spanish and the English connecting all the time."

## *El* Cowboy

The heyday of the American cowboy was roughly the last third of the nineteenth century. But the myth of the American cowboy lived on for decades after that. It still lingers, thanks in no small part to American movies and television. Now streaming: The Lone Star Channel.

With the myth come the inevitable myth-conceptions, and the Library of Congress punctures one of the biggest: the first cowboys were not Americans but Spanish. And joining them were Black cowboys.

Given that the Spanish introduced European horses to the Americas, where the native version had long since disappeared, that would seem to follow. But it wasn't what those cowboys were riding so much as what they were herding: cattle.

Thus, the name in Spanish for cowboy is *el vaquero,* from *vaca,* or cow. That morphed into **buckaroo,** a name for the American cowboy. In Spanish, the "v" in *vaquero* is pronounced like a "b," and for once, English went for the phonetic spelling. The editors at Dictionary.com advise that you're not apt to hear "buckaroo" much these days, but if you've ever wondered (because word persons wonder about these things) where "switcheroo" came from, as in the expression "the old switcheroo," we probably have the old buckaroo to thank for this slangy ending.

Back to those cowboys: those leather **chaps** that buckaroos wore over their pants were from the Spanish *chaparreras,* protective gear for the thick brush that they encountered. Some buckaroos also had **taps,** leather coverings for the stirrups on their saddle. This term is courtesy of *tapaderas,* which is related to those *tapas* that many of us enjoy nibbling. These, too, were originally coverings—for drinks glasses.

*Rodear* means "to surround," which is basically what happens in a **rodeo,** with the buckaroos using a knotted rope to **lasso** (*lazo*) a cow or horse. They do much the same when trying to rope in a wild *mestenco,* or **mustang.** Encounter enough of them and there could be a **stampede** (*estampida*).

Certain terms for Western terrain barely changed spelling from Spanish to English. *Cañón* became **canyon,** but **mesa** and **sierra** stayed just as they were. So did **corral** and **chaparral.** Just imagine translating the TV series *The High Chaparral* into *The High Impenetrable Thicket of Shrubs.*

On the subject of TV series—that ranch where Hoss and Little Joe hung out? Its name is from the Spanish for abundance and prosperity: **Bonanza.**

## Q: When Is a Gallon a Braid?

**A:** When you hear a word in Spanish to mean exactly the same as a word in English, even though your hearing may be a little off.

While it's true that in Spanish, *el galón* can mean a gallon the way it does in English, it can also mean a decorative braid.

This kind of *galón* sometimes encircled the hats the *vaqueros* wore, and there could be as many as ten such braids. To English-speaking ears, that amounted to—you guessed it—a **ten-gallon hat.**

## When Was the Last Time . . .

**. . . you went to a cafeteria for coffee?** In Mexican Spanish, *cafetería* literally means "coffee store." But it is rarely known as a destination for coffee, or *café*, because *-teria* came to mean the self-serve restaurants Americans know cafeterias to be. They first appeared in the US in the final years of the nineteenth century. Many businesses and factories adopted the idea for their workers.

**. . . you saw an armada safely crossing the road?** For most of us, the word "armada" calls to mind the Spanish warships that came to an ignominious end when they went up against England's Elizabeth I. But more than just naval ships, *armada* signifies an armed force, which is often encased in armor. The four-legged creature known as the **armadillo,**

with its protective casing, shares the Spanish *armado* in its name. But even with that armor, it has about the same luck crossing the road as the Spanish Armada did when it crossed Elizabeth.

# Five Wow Words from Spanish

The English versions are just a whisper away, if that, from their Spanish progenitors.

1. **aficionado.** English took the Spanish and ran with it, not changing a letter. Better than running with the bulls, often a prelude to a bullfight. The *Oxford English Dictionary* defines the English "aficionado" as first, "[a] devotee of bullfighting," and then, "by extension, an ardent follower of any hobby or activity."

 A **Meanderthal** *momento* regarding that bullfight: You know the English expression "moment of truth," meaning a turning point? It's actually translated from Spanish. As the language scholars Thomas Pyles and John Algeo explained in *The Origins and Development of the English Language*, its origin rests with what is often the demise of the bull. In *el momento de la verdad*, the bullfighter and the bull face off for the final outcome.

2. **picaresque.** A rascal, a rogue, a knave: the Spanish *picaresco* describes a *pícaro*, who could be a scoundrel or just a crafty soul. "Picaresque" is both noun and adjective in English, and a go-to word among literature mavens to describe the adventures of such a character. Huck Finn qualifies—though the word is far too fancy-pants for Twain's famous wanderer.

3. **lothario.** You might recognize the name from the— wait for it—picaresque seventeenth-century novel *Don*

*Quixote de la Mancha* by Miguel Cervantes. You might not, however, recognize it from a play written about one hundred years later titled *The Fair Penitent*. A ten-galón hat off to you if you know its British author: Nicholas Rowe. This was the work that forever branded a lothario as a shameless seducer of women.

4. **quixotic.** Of course, we can't mention that windmill tilter Don Quixote without bringing in this word that famously summons his name. Incurable romantics, hopeless idealists, soldiers who schlep to Kansas in search of gold—they're just begging to be called quixotic. But as O'Conner and Kellerman tell us, Spanish had *quijote* before it had Quixote. This *quijote* came from the French *cuisse* (just roll with that) and referred to protective armor for the thigh. Another armor story—and it seems like the Don could have done with more of it.

   We're not done yet. Among the volumes of writing that America's second president, John Adams, produced is this scathing comment about a Venezuelan general named Miranda who was plotting against Spain. "I considered Miranda as a vagrant," Adams all but spat, "a vagabond, a Quixotic adventurer." Adams was a pro at piercing a person's psychological armor with his verbal slings and arrows.

5. **mojito.** A popular rum-stoked cocktail whose birthplace is most often listed as Cuba, the Spanish verb *mojar* is often cited as its heritage. *Mojar* means to moisten or wet. While it would be tempting to link it with "wet your whistle," we'll avoid such a tangent, as it will have us meanderthalling waaay off course and going back to Chaucer. Besides, it's just plain wrong. But here's a Meanderthal *momentito* that is on track. The editors at the *Online Etymology Dictionary* point

out that *mojar* is connected to the Latin *mollire*, to soften. That takes us to "emollient," a soothing agent. Aficionados of the drink would likely agree with this assessment of a mojito.

## Looking Forward to a Snooze in the Sixth Hour?

While mad dogs and Englishmen go out in the midday sun, the Spanish, among others, are known to take an afternoon **siesta**, or nap, to get out of the midday sun. *Siesta* comes from the Latin *hora sexta*, meaning "sixth hour." Count six hours after dawn and it will bring you to around noontime, when the heat of the day is in high gear.

Now go have a siesta and then come back to read about cognates. Understood if you need a mojito for this next bit.

## Meet Your Kissin'-Cousin Cognates

Other than being one of the few pieces of linguist-speak populating these pages, just what are cognates, anyway? Here's how ACTFL, formerly the American Council on the Teaching of Foreign Languages, describes them: "Words between languages that have a common origin and are therefore readily understood." Just about every language that English has wed itself to has one or more of these relatives.

"Cognate," according to Pyles and Algeo, is from the Latin for "born together." One example in their book is the German *ergon* and the English *work*, both descendants of the Indo-European *\*wergom*. Just like family histories, cognates can get complicated. Anatoly Liberman, the author of *Word Origins and How We Know Them*, gives us these four German words: *lieben*, *vier*, *gehen*, and *Zahn*. Care to guess their English cognates? Love, four, go, and tooth.

But those examples are more like third cousins twice removed—cognates, you might say, only for those who are heavy-duty scholars. It's safe to finish that mojito now, because we're going to stick with the kissin'-cousin variety. They're more likely to look alike, even though they rarely sound exactly alike.

Consider the Spanish *el jardín* and the French *le jardin:* to look at 'em, they're identical twins, other than the articles. But the Spanish is pronounced "har-DEEN" and the French, "zhar-DEN." English steers clear of both, linking up instead with the German *Garten,* for "GAR-den." You'll probably recognize this *Garten* as the one in German's *Kindergarten*: lower that uppercase "K" and it's the English **kindergarten**.

## KISSIN' COUSINS FROM THE NORTH COUNTRIES

These English and Norwegian kissin' cousins come courtesy of a former instructor of Norwegian at Concordia Language Villages in Minnesota: *vinter* and winter, *regn* and rain, *katt* and cat.

Dutch does one better with *kat*/cat, and there's also *wolf*/wolf. And how about "bitter"? In Dutch, Norwegian, German, Danish, and Swedish, the word is exactly the same as in English, as the polymath J. Wes Ulm points out.

## SIDE-BY-SIDE-BY-SPANISH COGNATES

But it is with Spanish that English has a slew of linguistic cousins, running into the thousands. Andrew Barr, the founder of the Real Fast Spanish online learning program, offers an A-to-V list of one thousand plus one. He groups them into "perfect," the same spelling with the occasional accent for the Spanish, and "near perfect," where spellings somewhat differ.

Some of his "perfect" examples: *cerebral, familiar, gene, implacable, miserable, nostalgia, peculiar, secular, unión, versión.*

Barr's "near perfect" groupings reveal certain patterns that help native-English speakers (like Barr) feel at home with Spanish. A simple change in endings for a number of words, and you turn English into *español*.

Swap some English noun endings of "-tion" to *-ción* and look at that, they're Spanish:

- action to *acción*
- nation to *nación*

Swap some English adjective endings of "-ary" to *-ario*:

- contrary to *contrario*
- salary to *salario*

and "-ic" to *-ico:*

- electronic to *electrónico*
- fantastic to *fantástico*

There are still more patterns. Some "-ous" endings for English adjectives become Spanish when you swap them for *-oso—delicioso, precioso.* Ditto for "-ct" endings when they become *-cto—correcto, perfecto.*

## True or False? These Are All English-Spanish Kissin' Cousins

arena
brutal
central
cordial
enigma
mayor
medieval
regular
superficial

The answer is false, which you probably guessed, because word sleuths know a setup when they see one.

In fact, such interlopers are known in language lingo as false friends. They give the lie to the old saw about if it looks, walks, and quacks like a duck, it's a duck. In the case of false friends, this is quackery; the meanings of the words are completely different.

Now for the tougher quiz that you knew was coming: which words in the list are the false friends? Hint: there are two.

Give up?

*Arena* and *mayor.*

In Spanish, *arena* is sand, and *mayor* means older.

## The Poster Child of Spanish-English False Friends

There are plenty of these *gotcha!* words. *Actual* in Spanish actually means currently. Éxito means success. *Jubilación* means retirement (although many retirees may in fact be jubilant).

But the biggest *gotcha!* of them all is *embarazada.* It sure looks, walks, and quacks like "embarrassed," doesn't it? Let's just say there's a good chance that you will be embarrassed if you fall for this false friend: it means pregnant.

## Armor Again! Just One More Meanderthal...

Look how smoothly the word *armor* slides into **armoire.** Add an i and e, and *voilà!* We have the French word for cupboard (which English also latched onto), courtesy of the Latin *armarium.* The *arma* indicates weaponry, such as armor. So what's the connection to a cupboard?

We need to go back to long before Gutenberg fired up his printing press, when books were rare and monasteries were their keepers. "From the early tenth century," Judith Flanders tells us in *A Place for Everything,* "the Benedictines at Cluny Abbey in southeast France appointed an *armarius* to be in charge of the books—the *armarius* being responsible for the *armarium*, or cupboard, where the books were kept."

This abbey was not the only monastery that guarded its library in this way. In fact, according to the *Catholic Encyclopedia,* there was a popular saying of the time—in Latin, of course—that "a monastery without a library is like a fortress without an arsenal."

And what do you know? The Spanish word for weapon just happens to be—yep, *arma.*

# 16.
# AND THE GRAMMY GOES TO . . . GULLAH!

Actually, the Grammy Award went—twice—to Ranky Tanky, a band composed of five close friends from Charleston, South Carolina, for Best Regional Roots Music Album. Their music celebrates the Gullah Geechee community found along the southeastern coast of the US, from North Carolina to northern Florida, an area that enjoys the official congressional designation of the Gullah Geechee Cultural Heritage Corridor.

Gullah is both a culture and a language, one unique to the United States that found its voice in the eighteenth century. Some of the enslaved West Africans who were brought to the American South developed the language as a way to communicate with one another since their own, native tongues were multifarious. Their captors would select Africans who spoke different languages, betting that they would not be able to talk among themselves. The Babel-esque ruse backfired: a new, common language emerged instead.

## The only one of its kind

The coasts and tidal areas of South Carolina and Georgia in particular are home to many African Americans who are Gullah Geechee. The author Jessica Berry, who is a Gullah Geechee native of South Carolina, tells us that the words "Gullah" and "Geechee" may have derived from the names of two ethnic groups in Africa, the Gola and the Gidzi. "Gullah" is often attached to the Carolinas, and "Geechee" to Georgia and Florida.

In Gullah, "ranky tanky" means "get funky." Even if you're not familiar with this expression, there is a Gullah word—and song—you probably do know, as Ranky Tanky musician Charlton Singleton points out: **kumbaya.** It translates to "come by here."

If you are a lover of gospel music, a fan of R&B, or a devotee of what the documentary filmmaker Ken Burns describes as "one of the greatest exports we have"—jazz—then you have experienced Gullah. It occupies an unrivaled position in the E Pluribus pantheon as an English-based and African creole.

Somewhat like the languages it describes, the word **creole** has multiple roots: in French (*créole*), Spanish (*criollo*), and Portuguese (*crioulo*). Take these back to the Latin *creare* and you're practically at the English: to create or beget. A creole language is begat by mixing two or more languages.

Charles Joyner, a historian of the South who researched the Gullah language, maintained that in terms of African American culture, "the development of Gullah was comparable to the development of English, German, or French in the creation of these respective national cultures." And the same way that English brought in bundles of Romance-based words, Gullah harvested the English vocabulary, while following the sentence structure and grammatical features of West African languages.

For the second generation of Africans living in this part of America, says Virginia Mixson Geraty, the author of *Gulluh Fuh Oonuh (Gullah for You)*, Gullah became "their mother tongue."

## Up from Barbados, and back to Africa

Many of the enslaved Africans were brought first to Barbados, in the eastern Caribbean, before being shipped to South Carolina. Both were British strongholds at one time. The English-based Gullah creole that evolved in South Carolina and Georgia has echoes of the English-based Bajan creole of Barbados.

But the Gullah creole may well have roots in the very place from where its first speakers were uprooted: Africa. Historians such as Joseph Opala, and linguists such as John McWhorter, maintain that some of the enslaved would have been familiar with an English creole before they were taken from West Africa, since they would have been exposed to the "hybrid language," as Opala calls it, that British and African traders had established there.

## A slew and a stew

Even so, it is the prodigious slew of African languages that defines Gullah. The late Lorenzo Dow Turner, an African American who was both linguist and polyglot, traced four thousand-plus Gullah words and names, including phrases implanted in Gullah songs, back to various African languages. Turner was the first linguist to recognize Gullah as a language rather than some misguided version of English. His field work in the coastal communities of South Carolina and Georgia, along with his exhaustive research into the specific African languages embedded in Gullah, earned him the sobriquet of the "father of Gullah studies."

In 1949 Turner delivered this description of Gullah that was head-turning for its time:

> Gullah is a creolized form of English revealing survivals from many of the African languages spoken by the slaves who were brought to South Carolina and Georgia . . . These survivals are most numerous in the vocabulary . . . but can be observed also in its sounds, syntax, morphology, and intonation.

Listen to Gullah and you will hear: Fante, Fula, Ga, Igbo, Kimbundu, Malinke, Mandinka, Mende, Vai, Wolof, Yoruba, and more.

In Jessica Berry's *The Little Gullah Geechee Book,* she writes: "By taking pieces of their respective languages, traditions, and customs and mixing that with the language of the Buckra [the Gullah word for white man], my ancestors created a delicious stew of a culture, now known as Gullah Geechee."

Then she gives us a taste:

*Kiddy by da door.* (That's it, I'm done with you.)
*New broom sweep clean.* (Someone is taking over and will make changes.)
*I don't fool up with em.* (I don't get along with that person.)

## Born of a grain of rice

This "stew" was once as ubiquitous in Charleston, South Carolina, as the rice crop in the state's marshy Lowcountry. In fact, each fed the other.

"In the 1690s, a rice seed from Madagascar was introduced into the swamplands of the Charles Town colony," the linguists Tracey Weldon and Simanique Moody tell us. As a result of many more of those seeds being cultivated, the enslaved who worked in these swamplands made Charleston one of the world's wealthiest cities in the 1700s, and South Carolina the richest of the first thirteen colonies.

Many of the Africans taken captive were brought from West Africa specifically because of their skill in cultivating rice, a crop that for Africans held "sacred and ceremonial value," as the writer Angela Flournoy relays. So deep was their spiritual connection to this crop, she says, that some of the women were said to carry rice seeds with them in the braids of their hair. "They were smuggling nourishment of an existential kind."

The Africans who grew and harvested the rice in South Carolina often had little contact with their enslavers, who avoided the mosquito-riddled marshes. This imposed isolation, as Weldon and Moody point out, helped to keep the Gullah language intact. So did the large population of Africans working these rice fields. Contrast this with enslaved Blacks in New Jersey and New York, where there was no such separation from the enslavers. As a result, many of them, according to *The United States of English* author Rosemarie Ostler, spoke Dutch. Among them, according to another linguist, Ross Perlin, was Sojourner Truth.

*e pluribus* **ENGLISH**

## Deeply embedded

It is Gullah that prompted researchers in the South Carolina Sea Grant Consortium to note that "[p]erhaps more than any other American region, the South is a mix of African and European." Just consider the legume *Arachis hypogaea*, another food that traveled with the enslaved on the hellish voyage from Africa to America. It's commonly known as the peanut. But in the South, it's often known by the derivative of its African name of *nguba*: what speakers of Gullah—and speakers of Southern—call **goober**.

---

## The Big-Will Chill: African American English

Gullah is just one of the ways that African Americans made a language their own. In other parts of the South in the seventeenth and eighteenth centuries, captive Africans were more exposed to a variety of English—both British and Irish, as John McWhorter points out. As a result, English filtered more and more into the language of African Americans. And then the reverse happened: African American English, or AAE, filtered more and more into American English.

"Since the beginning of the twentieth century, African American English has had a steady influence on the vocabulary as a whole," writes Ostler, "although speakers sometimes don't recognize the cultural source of the words." It suffuses much of popular culture in America, as the linguist Chi Luu of the *JSTOR Daily* observes in her column, "sliding seamlessly into the language of art, music, poetry, storytelling, and social media."

Even if we are **dissing** a movie or a song, we are using a term made so popular by African American English, or AAE, that we pretty much dismiss the idea of using "dismissing" instead.

"Every speaker of American English borrows heavily from words invented by African Americans," maintains Henry Louis Gates, Jr. He is the director of Harvard's Hutchins Center for African & African American Research, but most of us know him as the force behind PBS's

*Finding Your Roots.* Here he is speaking in his capacity as editor-in-chief of the *Oxford Dictionary of African American English,* or *ODAAE,* which is as much the history of a unique American culture as it is a lively exploration of its words. A different way, you might say, of finding one's roots.

*Cool, hip, bad,* and *dig* are just a few of those words. In AAE, their meanings have nothing to do with temperature, limbs, naughtiness, or shovels. How about **grill** as a decorative dental overlay, and **kitchen** as the hair at the back of the neck? Both words made the cut of the first one hundred words that the Dictionary presented.

Gates compares the way that African American English reimagines the language to "the way Louis Armstrong took the trumpet and turned it inside out from the way people played European classical music."

H'mmm. Doesn't this remind you, being the alert reader that you are, of someone we met across the Pond way back in the early 1600s? Yes, that Shakespeare fellow. He invigorated the language by finding fresh ways to use many words that were already in the English lexicon. The speakers of AAE do much the same. "Hustle," for example, has been around as a verb since the late seventeenth century, but it was African American English that delivered **side hustle.** "Cake" is another example.

While Shakespeare, as we learned, popularized "cake" as a verb, speakers of AAE kept the noun but took its meaning beyond the literal. Behold **cakewalk**, which now describes something easily accomplished. The word grew out of a contest, often perfunctory, that Blacks took part in pre-Emancipation. For the Black couples who executed the most stylized walk, their prize was a cake.

And then there's "chill." As a verb meaning to become cold, it's been around longer than Big Will Shakespeare, dating to the 1300s. But it's AAE that made it even cooler, as a punchier way to say "relax." Just **chill.**

# Four African Words You Didn't Know You Knew

"The American nation is in a sense the product of the American language," wrote the novelist Ralph Ellison in a 1970 essay. "It is a language that began by merging the sounds of many tongues, brought together in the struggle of diverse regions. And whether it is admitted or not, much of the sound of that language is derived from the timbre of the African voice and the listening habits of the African ear."

Here are four words from African languages. Can you guess what they became in English? The answers follow, in sequence. Bet you'll figure them out before you reach that point.

1. **Banaana.** It's from Wolof, and was first funneled through Spanish (*banana*) and Portuguese (*banana*) before it arrived in English.
2. **Tamgu.** You can find several stories about the origin of *tamgu*. In Ibibio, the word means "to dance." The editors at the *Online Etymology Dictionary* posit that the word came to describe an African and South American dance done to drums. Finish this expression and you'll have the answer: "It takes two to _____."
3. **Mgombo.** Speaking of drums, this is a Bantu word that means just that. The first music to be made with the *mgombo* was in Cuba, where the Spanish called it *el bongó*.
4. **Nyami.** This Fulani word means "to eat." But it morphed into the name of a particular food in Africa, one that was especially nourishing and that Europeans readily scooped up. The Portuguese called it *inhame* and the Spanish, *ñame*. English kept it simple—and kept the "y."

Answers: **banana, tango, bongo,** and **yam.**

# Where There Is Mojo, There Once Was Indigo

"Got my **mojo** working," sang the blues artist Muddy Waters back in the 1950s. Except that in this song, this nearly magical brand of self-confidence didn't seem to work on the woman he wanted.

By then, "mojo" had come to suggest the kind of positive attraction that most of us associate with the word. Seasonings, spices, cosmetics, hair care—"mojo" finds its way into the names of all kinds of products today. But the original brand of magic, or *moco* in Gullah, was deployed as a deterrent. (*Moco* is also close to *moco'o*, according to the etymologist Ben Zimmer, a West African word for "medicine man.") Carrying a mojo—an amulet, or a small bag of herbs—guarded against evil spirits known as **hants**. Think "haunt" and you're there.

One of the most powerful mojos was a certain color blue.

In addition to being expert at rice propagation, the West Africans enslaved in South Carolina's Lowcountry were superior at cultivating indigo plants, a valuable commodity in the eighteenth century. The Gullah Geechee could not share in this wealth; nevertheless, they would mix the dregs of the indigo dye with lighter pigments that formed a blue-green color. This became known as **haint blue**. (Here again, think "haunt.")

"The Geechee believed that the color mimicked blue water and blue sky which tricked the spirits . . . therefore painting a porch, window, or door 'haint blue' meant spirits couldn't make their way into your home," explains Bilal Morris, who covers Black folklore for NewsOne.

Today, homes primarily in the South with a haint blue hue are still easy to spot, and major paint companies offer colors that summon this mojo and its history.

e pluribus **ENGLISH**

## How Juke Joints and Banjos Forever Changed the Music

If you've read James McBride's *The Heaven & Earth Grocery Store*, you've come across references to juke joints (or jook, as he spells it). The word "jukebox" grew out of this. Both relate to music—a certain type of music establishment (the joint), a particular way to listen to music (the box).

Dr. Lorenzo Turner, in studying the Gullah word *juk*, traced **juke** back to two West African languages. One is Bambara, where *jugu* describes a devilish person; the other is Wolof, where *jug* indicates an unruly life.

But once in America, "juke" acquired a more positive spin. A juke joint became both refuge and incubator—a refuge where newly freed Blacks throughout the South could socialize and enjoy music, and an incubator of one genre of music in particular: the blues.

The jukebox was originally called "nickel-in-the-slot phonograph." The name didn't catch on (imagine), but the idea of a coin-operated music player in diners where patrons could select the songs they wanted to hear became entrenched in twentieth-century American culture. The iPod may have been sleeker, but the jukebox never really lost its clunky cachet.

As early as the 1600s, Blacks in the Caribbean were strumming a **banjo**, and by the next century they had brought it to America. The word traces its roots to Angola and the Bantu language known as Kimbundu, where Africans referred to a similar instrument as *mbanza*. Originally, those who played the banjo plucked strings across a gourd covered with animal skin.

Once entrenched in America, the banjo became the musical backdrop of dances such as the Virginia Reel. But the instrument soon took center stage in an iconic African American musical genre: ragtime. As the Oxford African American Studies Center relays: "Most ragtime popular songs were published with banjo arrangements, and ragtime composers like [Scott] Joplin dedicated scores to black banjoists and annotated their piano scores with instructions for the pianist to play like a banjoist."

## Gullah in Literature

**Q:** What well-known author tried to incorporate Gullah into a story?

- Mark Twain
- Edgar Allen Poe
- Herman Melville

**A:** Poe, in his short story "The Gold-Bug," from 1843. He used South Carolina's Sullivan's Island, where many Gullah Geechee lived, as the setting.

## Shout and *Sha'wt*

**Shout-out** is an AAE expression that has "crossed over" into American English, as Tracey Weldon, an executive editor of the *ODAAE*, says. But **ring shout**, also an AAE expression, is not as common outside the Black community.

Like cakewalk, ring shout involves a dance—but this time, a spiritual one. It dates back to the original Gullah Geechee, who often spontaneously performed the dance in "praise houses." These were small, tucked-away structures that were safe havens for prayers. Participants in a ring shout move counterclockwise in a circle—the ring—clapping as they chant and sing.

Which makes it easy to assume that the "shout" refers to this singing and chanting . . . although it may not.

Along with other captive Africans, some of the Gullah had been Muslim when they were taken from their homeland. An Arabic word for the counterclockwise religious movement that Muslims would engage in as part of a religious rite is *sha'wt*. In English, the pronunciation is close to "shout."

e pluribus **ENGLISH**

## A President, a Queen, and Hip-Hop

In early January 2009, President-elect Barack Obama dropped into a popular diner in Washington, DC, for some smoked sausage and sweet tea. When the cashier tried to give him his change for the order, Obama waved it off. "Nah," he said, "we straight." Obama was speaking African American English, which more Americans would come to hear more often.

Two years later, President and Mrs. Obama were staying in the stately Buckingham Palace as a guest of the Queen, whom they both took a shine to. Obama's national security advisor, Ben Rhodes, was with them. In a memoir Rhodes later penned, he recalled joking with the president that perhaps they were witnessing "a dying empire." The President disagreed. "Did you see the bling on the Queen?" This time, Obama's lively riposte was thanks to a word from rap.

**Bling,** a term birthed in rap music, is now so ubiquitous that you'd think the word had been around forever. But it's only been since the 1990s that we've been hearing this as a description of flashy jewelry. You might have heard the more onomatopoeic "bling-bling" at times as well. Either way, what you're hearing is the word of a rapper.

UCLA professor of English Adam Bradley, founding director of the university's Laboratory for Race and Popular Culture, is also an advisory board member for the *Oxford Dictionary of African American English*. He places the birth of "bling" (the song, not the thing) to 1999 in New Orleans, with the rappers Y.G. and Lil Wayne.

"Bling" became so popular that it landed in the *Oxford English Dictionary* in the early aughts of this century. It's also in *Merriam-Webster,* among other dictionaries. Bradley jokes that even his grandmother caught on to it.

Are you **woke**, in the sense of being aware of societal issues ("especially," adds *Merriam-Webster* parenthetically, "issues of racial and social justice")? The word can be either complimentary or derogatory, depending on the speaker's inclination. Either way, it's hip-hop—although, as Bradley points out, "you can trace its use in Black popular song much further back than that." To 1938, in fact, when the blues singer Lead Belly used it in his song *Scottsboro Boys*.

Have you ever been **ghosted**? Thank hip-hop (for the term, not the act). Here again, just as with Big Will, "ghost" has been around since the days of the Old English noun *gāst*, but it got a new life, and meaning, as a verb.

As Bradley observed during the panel discussion on hip-hop and rap's influence on language and culture that the *ODAAE* recorded in the fall of 2024, "Rap is a powerful means of amplifying language—sometimes inventing or innovating, but the amplification is really key."

# 17.
# BEIGNETS, GRIEF BACON, AND BAGELS

French, German, and Yiddish words all took up residence in American English. The first waves of its speakers still whisper in our ears, even with the many new waves of speakers who later took up residence in the same parts of America. Imagine Louisiana with no French, southeastern Pennsylvania minus German, and the Lower East Side of Manhattan at the turn of the twentieth century devoid of Yiddish. As Henry Hitchings pronounces in *The Secret Life of Words*, "the bilingualism of many Americans has impregnated American English with the exotic."

## *French*

### Déjà vu all over again

Like Spanish, French left an indelible impression on American English. There was the French of the Northwest and the Midwest, of trappers and traders—of **butte** and **prairie, crevasse** and **cache**, the latter being places where trappers hid their secret stash of supplies.

Before it was the Land of 10,000 Lakes (or, as one resident joked, of ten thousand Olsens), Minnesota was a land of French speakers. French explorers and traders were there as early as 1659, according to Mark Labine, a longtime member of the French-American Heritage Foundation, whose ancestry dates back to the earliest French settlers in Minnesota. Cities such as Duluth, La Salle, and Joliet carry the names of these traders. And the state motto? *L'etoile du Nord*, or North Star.

Minnesota is not alone in its plethora of French place-names. *Ouisconsin* is how Colleen Leahy of Wisconsin Public Radio playfully introduced her segment on French names in that state. At one time, the "Wis" in Wisconsin was in fact pronounced like *oui* in French. Prairie du Sac, Prairie du Chien, Presque Isle, Portage: all are place-names in Oui/Wisconsin. They join our new friend butte, this time in Butte des Morts, probably best left in its original French, as it translates to "mound of the dead."

## 'Pardon me, Lord, parlez-vous anglais?'

The French also settled in New England, from Maine south to Connecticut. Among the first wave were those from southeastern Canada who were expelled from Acadia in the early 1700s, when the British wrested the territory from France and renamed it Nova Scotia. Few if any of the Catholic French wished to convert to the British Protestantism and so were deported.

Later, other groups of French Canadians continued the exodus to New England, working in the region's many textile mills in the nineteenth and early twentieth centuries and making pockets of the region wealthy in the process. Language borrowing occurred here, too, but not much of it, and in the reverse. French-speaking workers in the mill towns of New Hampshire were known to adapt a few English words to express some mill terms—turning "spinner" and "weaver," for example, from nouns into verbs. And that was about it.

Jesse Martineau, who became a member of the New Hampshire House of Representatives in 2016, and his sister, Monique Cairns, grew up in Manchester, one of New Hampshire's mill towns. They recall that the city's French community was linguistically self-sufficient: no English needed.

Their parents attended what today would be called a dual language school, half the day in French and half in English. "This was not uncommon in New England," they point out. What amused Martineau, though, was that only two subjects were taught in French: the French language and the Catholic religion. "My parents joke it was not until they were older that it even occurred to them that God might be able to understand English."

## From Bayeux to bayou

It was when the French language went south, to where the Mississippi River meets the Gulf of Mexico, that more of it flowed into English.

Not all of the expelled Acadians settled in New England. Some headed to Louisiana, to be known from then on as Cajuns. Their Cajun French was just one of the French dialects that would shape this state, where counties are called parishes, portions of the law derive from the Napoleonic Code, and the state is a member of the International Organization of La Francophonie. Louisiana Creole, also known as Kouri Vini, is a rich dish of African and Caribbean linguistic influences mixed with French. And some Indigenous groups incorporate their own variations of French into their tribal language.

Georgie V. Ferguson, a member of the Pointe-au-Chien, says that his tribe "has one of the most distinct and identifiable dialects of spoken French in Louisiana." What you hear in it, he explains, is "an amalgamation of traditional Indian words incorporated from the Indigenous languages traditionally spoken by our ancestors."

One of the words that is practically synonymous with Louisiana is **bayou.** Yes, it's courtesy of the French, in an effort to describe a body of water somewhere between a creek and a swamp. But the French had to do some borrowing, too—from the Choctaw *bayuk*, meaning small stream.

French is not the only language of influence in Louisiana today. Spanish, in fact, surpasses it, and Vietnamese is right behind French. But so diverse are the ways that French has taken hold that there is a dictionary devoted just to the French of the region. *The Dictionary of Louisiana French* features the French of Cajun, Creole, and Indigenous groups in the Bayou State.

## Words that English just ate right up

French in Louisiana is also emblematic of how many food names of other cultures feed the English language. For the most part, they have survived intact, with English—particularly American English, given the country's many cultures—gobbling up their original spelling, even if the pronunciation gets a bit mangled. We don't even blink at the Polish *pierogi,* the Italian *tiramisu,* the Korean *kimchi,* or the Vietnamese *pho.*

Some of the earliest such words in America are courtesy of French and the food culture of New Orleans. Test your NOLA (New Orleans, LA) knowledge in the first two vignettes.

## Of Cabbages and Kings

Here are clues to five foodie French words that are very familiar if you live in New Orleans or have visited there, and worth guessing if you haven't.

1. Belgium, France, and New Orleans all claim this creation as theirs. All three are correct, as each concocts a different version of it. In New Orleans, it was African American women who made it a delectation unique to the Crescent City (so nicknamed because of how the Mississippi curves around the city). France can claim the word origin, often maintaining it's named after a count. The food found its way into a book of *receipts*—what we know as recipes—as early as 1714. Some say you'd have to be nuts not to love it (unsubtle hint for you).

## e pluribus ENGLISH

2. It's a mishmash of meat or seafood or both, either with tomatoes (Creole "red") or without (Cajun "brown"), but always with rice. Both the dish and the word reflect a mishmash of cultures, including Spanish and African as well as French. "Mishmash," by the way, was the word's original meaning in Provençal French. Hint: the Spanish have a comparable dish called paella.
3. Suffocate, choke, stifle, throttle: these are all synonyms for the literal translation of the name of this dish. Rest assured that none of these unpleasantries befall you when you enjoy the main ingredient—traditionally crawfish, or *ecrevisse*—that is smothered in a thick broth and simmered. This French term describes both the dish and its cooking technique and is not the only one. **Fricassee** is another, possibly its own mix of the French words for fry and cut up. **Rotisserie** is one more, from the French verb for roasting.
4. The Old French word for this meant "lump," which hardly does justice to this popular breakfast square (hint, hint). The Celtic *bigne*, meaning "to raise," also played a part. The French were no doubt enjoying some version of this raised lump for centuries before it became a New Orleans mainstay.
5. The fact that its origin is from a French word meaning to knead is a giveaway. What makes this a New Orleans standout is its role in Carnival and its ubiquitous king cake, long a fixture in France and other parts of Europe. The ring-shaped cake dates back to Roman times, the "king" signifying the Feast of the Three Kings celebrated on January 6th. This is the start of Carnival.

**Answers:**
1. **Praline.** This nutty, sugary confection is pronounced "PRAH-leen" in New Orleans. Some also pronounce it **decadent**, another word with French ancestry that suggests falling or sinking. This has yet to deter those who have fallen for this sweet.

2. **Jambalaya.** The word may be French but the dish shares a long history with a kingdom in West Africa called the Jolof, or Wolof, Empire. This is the same Wolof as the language that echoes in Gullah. It is also the same Jolof of jollof rice, the African dish that features meats and tomatoes and inspired jambalaya.
3. **Étouffée.** The hint, by the way, was "smothered," the literal meaning of étouffée. And if by chance you're wondering what the difference is between crawfish and crayfish, it's one of latitude: craw in the South, cray in the North.
4. **Beignet.** Often described as a doughnut, albeit with no hole, the beignet has a propensity to puff up, thanks to its **choux** pastry. Choux is from the French *pâte à choux*—literally, cabbage pastry. Nothing to do with the taste, thank goodness, just the resemblance that this light dough has to tiny cabbages.
5. **Brioche.** The classic Mardi Gras king cake is made with brioche dough. The bread's sweeter taste lands somewhere between a more traditional bread and a cake. The distinction places it in the realm of a *viennoiserie*, a term the French coined to describe baked goods like those found in Vienna: part bread, part pastry. That term may not be overly familiar, but along with brioche, another well-known indulgence fits the bill: **croissant**, so named for its crescent shape.

# Next on the NOLA Menu: Haitian Creole

The people who settled in New Orleans from Haiti, once the French colony of Saint-Domingue, brought their own version of the French language, called Haitian Creole. They also brought the flavors of their

Caribbean island, many of them the forerunners of the tastes of New Orleans today.

While *voodoo* and *zombie* are Haitian Creole words familiar to English speakers, many of the food names are not as well-known beyond NOLA and fans of the former TV show *Treme*. Not yet, anyway. Here are a few to chew on:

**fritai**. Fried street food.
**gratine**. Macaroni and cheese with ground beef.
**pikliz**. Spicy relish.
**griot**. Pork chunks marinated in citrus, first braised and then fried.
**diri kole**. Rice and beans. Literally, "stuck together."

## The Lowdown on Levee

Bet you don't wake up quite like Louis XIV of France did: with a group of distinguished subjects ready to greet their Sun King right in his bedroom. *Lever* in French means "to raise," and as Ben Zimmer tells us, when it involved Louis, that extended to the idea of rise-and-shine. Soon comparable *levées*, or receptions, caught on with important people on both sides of the Pond, although not in their bedrooms.

But just a few years after Louis's death in 1715, Zimmer notes, French cartographers who were mapping the new city of New Orleans were using *la levée* in a very different way: to indicate a raised embankment for containing rising water.

"An English-language map of the time gave it a wordier designation," Zimmer tells us, and a prescient one at that: "'Bank to preserve the Town from the Inundation.'"

##  Meanderthal Morsel: Holy Trinity

Much like many Native Americans have "three sisters" when it comes to food (squash, corn, and beans), Cajun and Creole dishes have celery, bell pepper, and onion, a threesome known as the holy trinity. Paul Prudhomme, the celebrity Cajun chef, popularized the term, drawing from the familiar Christian triad of Father, Son, and Holy Spirit: the Holy Trinity.

## *German*

### It's making down some Deutsch treats

The Germans who settled in parts of Pennsylvania starting in the seventeenth century spoke their own brand of their native tongue called Pennsylfawnisch. That didn't catch on with English ears, but "Pennsylvania Dutch" did. There was just one **glitch** (to borrow from the Yiddish, as the late astronaut John Glenn did when describing a technical hiccup with Project Mercury in 1962). The language wasn't Dutch at all, it was German—or *Deutsch*. Nevertheless, the glitch stuck.

These early German arrivals also practiced their own brand of religion, much like the Puritans, which is why "Amish" is sometimes used interchangeably with "Pennsylvania Dutch." Certain expressions are hallmarks of these speakers—like "it's making down" (it's coming down) for a pelting rain and "eat yourself done" (eat up).

### Scraps and fasts

As for eating yourself done, two of several well-known Pennsylvania Dutch dishes are **scrapple** and **fasnacht**.

Scrapple, as the word suggests, involves cooking leftover scraps of pork in cornmeal (originally) or flour. It's not a dish these Deutsch's relatives across the Pond knew, even though the Penn Dutch used the German for leftover: *pănhās,* or variations thereof. That seems a long way, though, from "scrapple." Some say the full German name of what resembled a meatloaf was *panhaskroppe,* which comes closer.

Fasnacht is an annual one-off of sweet(ish) fried dough made with potato flour. One enjoys it right before Lent starts. In other words, on the night (*nacht*) before fasting (*fasten*) begins.

## Scissors and spritz

Like fasnacht, some other Penn Dutch words will have you speaking German in no time, because you practically are.

**Scherenschnitte** is the craft of cutting paper into complex patterns, which is harder to do than even remembering how to spell this word. But *scheren* is German for scissors, and *schnitt* for cut, so really, what could be more clear-cut?

**Snollygoster** suggests a slick and savvy individual who is not on a first-name basis with scruples. The word's origin is equally slippery, but it's mighty close to *schnelle geeschter,* meaning "quick spirits."

If you use the Penn Dutch *verhuddle* when things are in a muddle, native-English listeners might be confused by what you're saying. Say it in English instead: **ferhoodle**, which means to confuse.

There's no confusion, though, with these three Penn Dutch words: **spritz** (*spritzen*), **dunk** (*dunke*), and **ouch,** which is quite possibly from the PD *outch* and most probably from the German *autsch.* The *OED* dates the earliest example of "ouch" in written form to 1838, in a work by an American humorist living in Pennsylvania. Along with "ouch" being the interjection that comes not to mind but straight out of our mouths when, say, we drop a pair of scissors on our toe, it has also become a nifty little put-down when someone insults us—say, when they criticize our attempts at scherenschnitte.

## What Harm in Such Joy?

Many more German words made their way into English besides those from Pennsylvania Dutch. There are the usual suspects, among them: *hamburger, dachshund, rathskeller, Bauhaus, über, umlaut* (the diacritical double dots above the u in über). And a word that caught on in English faster than you can say *sauerkraut* (also German): **schadenfreude.** It's a sophisticated-sounding word for reveling in another's misery; we first met up with it at the start of the book. *Schaden* means harm or damage, and *freude* means joy. Seldom have two seeming contradictions worked so well together.

It's hardly the only such German word that in most cases we brought lock, stock, and spelling into English, and that do a dandy job of describing . . . whatever it is they're describing.

Think of a particular outlook, such as **wanderlust** and **zeitgeist**, and also **gestalt**. How about a literary or thematic device, like **bildungsroman** or **leitmotif**? Someone you've seen—**doppelgänger**—or not—**poltergeist**. A way of seeing the world—**Weltanschauung**—and a way of being in it—**gemütlichkeit**.

English is, after all, a Germanic language, so maybe that's why we don't blink at these multisyllabic marvels.

The nine words just mentioned reveal their meanings in much the same way as schadenfreude. What follows is the translation of the first part of each word; see if you can pick the second part from these clues: **novel, pleasure, goer, positive, view, motive, spirit.**

**Tips:** one word has no second part, and two words have the same.

*Wanderlust*: to wander + _____
*Zeitgeist*: time + _____
*Gestalt*: shape or form + _____
*Bildungsroman*: education or growth + _____
*Leitmotif*: to lead + _____

*Doppelgänger:* double + _____
*Poltergeist:* to knock + _____
*Weltanschauung:* world + _____
*Gemütlichkeit:* disposition + _____

**Answers:**
Wander lust: to wander + **pleasure**
Zeit geist: time + **spirit**
Gestalt: shape or form
Bildungs roman: education or growth + **novel**
Leit motif: to lead + **motive**
Doppel gänger: double + **goer**
Polter geist: to knock + **spirit**
Welt anschauung: world + **view**
Gemüt lich keit: disposition + **positive** (+ feeling, for extra points)

## It's in the Cards

What do **pinochle** and **kaput** have in common? Not much as far as how English uses them. But they both came to English via German, and both origins started with French card games.

"Pinochle" derived from the German card game *Binokel;* that in turn is connected to the French card game of *bezique.* "Kaput," which has nothing to do with a card game anymore, started out as part of the expressions used in the French card game of *piquet* to indicate both winning big and losing mightily: *capot* in French. That evolved into *kaputt* in German, which was reserved just for the losers.

## If the Glue Sticks

In Daniel Mason's novel *North Woods*, an eighteenth-century artist pens his dismay to a friend back in the city on how his newly purchased country house has withstood a series of ad hoc additions over the century. "Out here," he writes, "no one tears down anyway—one just adds upon, *agglutinates*, house to house . . . like some monstrous German noun."

"Agglutinate" and "glue" share the same Latin ancestry. But it's German that knows how to take a string of letters and make them stick. Such words bring a pronounced heft to English, even if they don't quite go trippingly on the tongue of a native-English speaker the way they do on a German's. So why not add some more of them to our everyday—okay, maybe every other day—conversations? It just might be *Eigenzeit*, or the proper time. For example, it's about time we had a word that falls somewhere between "instinct" and "tact," and what says it better than *Fingerspitzengefühl*, or "finger tips feeling"? (Hey, *The New Yorker* used it.)

Here are five more agglutinates that caught the ear of Emma Anderson of FluentU after living in Germany for five years:

1. *Fremdscham:* Cringing on behalf of someone who's doing something cringeworthy.
2. *Torschlusspanik:* That distressed feeling when it dawns on us that something significant is disappearing. So book that vacation of a lifetime before *Torschlusspanik* sets in.
3. *Erklärungsnot:* You've been caught in the act, and now you must explain yourself—and fast.
4. *Verschlimmbessern:* Making things worse instead of better.
5. *Schnapsidee:* It sure *sounded* like a good idea after that third swig of schnapps last night.

One more that is just too good to not agglutinate into English: **Kummerspeck.** It's what can happen when we eat our way out of feeling low and see the scale go higher as a result. But there's a more amusing way to remember its meaning—by what it loosely translates to, which is "grief bacon."

## *Yiddish*

### How Americans Learned to Nosh

In Yiddish, English shares a sliver, or **shtikl,** of common history: both began as Germanic languages (Yiddish around 1000 CE), although Yiddish uses a Hebrew alphabet. Also much like English, Yiddish absorbed elements of the various languages that European Jews came in contact with, both in western and eastern Europe.

Eastern European Jews escaping the Russian **pogroms** of the late nineteenth and early twentieth centuries ("pogrom" being Russian for "wreaking havoc") looked west to the Americas. By the mid-1920s, more than a million Jews who spoke Yiddish had arrived in New York City and quickly came to define Manhattan's Lower East Side. Yiddish theater and newspapers proliferated; the largest paper, *Forverts (Forward),* is still publishing.

Yiddish, which translates to "Jewish," is both language and culture, and the *mamaloshen*, or mother tongue, of Europe's Ashkenazi Jews. During the last hundred years, it has waned and waxed in America following its apogee in the 1920s. Globally, the Holocaust silenced at least half of all Yiddish voices. But today, Yiddish is once again thriving in New York—this time in the borough of Brooklyn, as a Hasidic language.

The linguist Ross Perlin marvels at the rebirth in his book *Language City* (welcome to New York). "Immigrant languages in America rarely last beyond the third generation," he writes, "but the Hasidim are now passing on Yiddish to a fifth . . . achieving what arguably only rural Old Order Amish and Mennonites have achieved with Pennsylvania Dutch."

The late Isaac Bashevis Singer, recipient of the 1978 Nobel Prize in Literature, both spoke and wrote in Yiddish. He once observed in his wry, wonderful way that Yiddish was "perhaps the only language never spoken by men in power."

Yet it wields a power all its own. You'd be hard-pressed to find native-English speakers in the US who don't reach for Yiddish, even when they have no idea they're doing so. Like this: "*Ich darf es vi a loch in kop*." Don't know it? Yeah, you do: "I need this like a hole in the head."

## 'As American as Bagels and Rice Krispies'

We have the editors of *How Yiddish Changed America and How America Changed Yiddish,* Ilan Stavans and Josh Lambert, to thank for this memorable description of Yiddish culture and language in America.

Um ... Rice Krispies?

It's a bit of a gobsmacker for those of us who don't know the history but makes perfect sense for those who do. The snap-crackle-pop cereal is a popular base for hamantasch, the triangular pastry that is a mainstay of the Purim holiday.

Bagels, of course, need no explanation. As Stavans and Lambert tell us, "In the twentieth century, delicatessens became staples of every major American city, and bagels triumphed across the country."

And riding high on that victory was a **schmear**, or spread, of cream cheese.

## Ten to Try

Why ...
1. ... snack when you can **nosh.**
2. ... complain when you can **kvetch.**
3. ... exult when you can **kvell.**
4. ... fiddle around when you can **futz.**
5. ... glad-hand when you can **schmooze.**
6. ... nag when you can **noodge.**
7. ... be clumsy when you can be a **klutz.**
8. ... plop when you can **plotz.**
9. ... dismiss it as dross when you can disparage it as **dreck.**
10. ... call a namby-pamby a wuss when you can call this nervous Nellie a **nebbish.**

# e pluribus ENGLISH

## Role Reversal: English to Yiddish

Before Ellis Island became the gateway for immigrants to America, a fort at the foot of Manhattan with the improbable name of Castle Garden served as the point of entry during the mid- to late-nineteenth century. The millions of immigrants landing there made it a busy, noisy place. It inspired the American Yiddish coining of *keslgarten* to describe, as Ross Perlin writes, "any chaotic and confusing place."

## Yes I Said Yes I Will Schlep

No greater a word **maven** (yes, it's Yiddish: from *mevyn*, denoting a knowledgeable person) than James Joyce commandeered **schlep** in his *Ulysses*. "She trudges, schlepps, trains, drags, trascines her load," he wrote. It's a veritable thesaurus of a sentence that describes lugging a load, delivered with a certain **chutzpah,** or confidence in the extreme.

The *sch* in schlep shows up in a number of other Yiddish words, and in places besides Joyce's Dublin. Like a Milwaukee brewery and the two ever-striving, always-stumbling characters who schlep to their jobs there. By now you may have already summoned the theme song of the sitcom *Laverne and Shirley,* where the two belt out **"Schlemiel, schlemizal."** Both Yiddishisms, schlemiel suggests inept and schlemizal, unlucky. But Barry Kibrick of PBS reaches for the Yiddish saying that says it better: "A schlemiel is somebody who often spills his soup, and a schlimazel is the person it lands on." *Laverne and Shirley*'s **schtick**, or routine (from the German for slice), stuck with viewers, even if not everybody got the joke.

Two more from the *sch* pantheon for you: **schnoz** and **schmaltz.** They have to do with a dog and a chicken. Like so: Schnoz is slang for a big nose and derives from the German *shnauze,* or snout, the very same that gives us *schnauzer*. Schmaltz in its purest sense means melted animal fat, usually from a chicken. But schmaltz has also become shorthand for a surfeit of sentimentality. Hey, a little schmaltz can do us all good. To borrow another Yiddish phrase: "Okay by me."

# 18.
# "A LANGUAGE CANNOT BE TOO RICH"

"I am of the opinion that our tung should be written cleane and pure, vnmixt and vnmangled with borowing of other tunges," pronounced a sixteenth-century royal tutor and courtier. Oh, and in case it needs to be said: an Englishman.

It was not to be. English became, in the eyes and ears of some, not only mangled but tangled with too many newfangled words.

## Belittle *that*

Shakespeare, as we saw, was the poster boy for neologisms on one side of the Pond; Thomas Jefferson was among the wannabes on the other.

"I set equal value on the beautiful engraftments we have borrowed from Greece and Rome; and I am equally a friend to the encouragement of a judicious Neology, a language cannot be too rich," Jefferson wrote.

But when Jefferson introduced "belittled," according to Rosemarie Ostler, the Brits did just that: they dissed it. English English and American English would start to part ways on many words. Where EE has dustbin, AE has wastebasket. Ditto for windscreen/windshield, lorry/truck, trolly/cart, among others.

The same might be said of flat/apartment and autumn/fall. Except that it would be incorrect. At one time EE also used "apartment" and "fall," according to *Origins of the Specious* authors O'Conner and Kellerman. "Americans have saved many, many words that the English have lost," they inform us rather solemnly. Pulled them right out of that dustbin.

On the other hand, as *The Secret Life of Words* author Henry Hitchings points out, "American English has lost *fortnight*." For all this, the two Englishes have continued to add words to the hoard. As Hitchings reminds us, "American English and British English are adjacent parts of the big continuum of intelligibility known simply as 'English'."

## The bento and the octopus

Contrast the English propensity to collect with the Japanese proclivity to compartmentalize. The Japanese use a sort of linguistic bento box to keep words that have entered their language (other than Chinese) in their own separate spot. They created a separate writing script, called katakana, to corral all those imports to their language and keep them in one place. Katakana serves other purposes as well, but containing these non-Japanese words is an important function.

"Since the Second World War, the ever-growing range of foreign-imposed vocabulary has been derived overwhelmingly from English," observes Polly Barton, an Englishwoman who spent her first year as a Cambridge University graduate teaching English on Japan's Sado Island in 2005. Two such examples in her book, *Fifty Sounds*, are *howaitobōdo* and *shītoberuto*, katakana for "whiteboard" and "seat belt."

Compare this insular, arms-close-to-the-chest approach with English, as shape-shifting as an octopus, its arms ever reaching for more words. No bento box for this beast. "Of all the world's languages English was already the most checkered, the most mottled, the most polygenetic," writes James Gleick in *The Information*. "Its history showed continual corruption and enrichment from without." And Gleick was writing about the English of the early 1600s. In this regard—the checkered, mottled, polygenetic part—English has been nothing if not steadfast over the centuries. But note how Gleick has "corruption" and "enrichment" rubbing shoulders with each other. Bring on those other tunges.

## Sparking joy in the palimpsest

If we were to give Gleick's description a bit of a PR spin, we might say that English is like a **palimpsest**. The word is from the Greek *palimpsēstos*, meaning "scraped again." It originally referred to scraping writing off parchment, a precursor to paper, to reuse it for new writing. What had gone before was often gone for good, or a shadow of itself. English is like a self-repeating palimpsest, adding and adding, but seldom subtracting. It is the anti-Marie Kondo of languages. And Japanese is among the languages that have sparked joy in English.

The *OED* tells us that English has more than five hundred Japanese loanwords. *Bento, tatami,* and *shogun* were some of the earliest, from the 1600s. English stuck with just **shogun** (military commander) rather than *sei-i taishōgun*, which the etymologist John Kelly of Mashed Radish explains is "a fuller title that can be literally translated as 'barbarian-conquering great general.'" In case you ever need to put a finer point on it.

*Tofu* was corrupting and enriching in the next century, along with *samurai* and *koi*. By the late 1800s, English had *sushi* and *shiitake* and *matcha*, even if these tunges were not yet familiar tastes on the English tongue.

## Haiku and honchos

The American poet Ezra Pound tried his hand in 1913 at a "hokku-like sentence"—aka **haiku**—another Japanese word brought into English in the late 1800s. Decades later, Jack Kerouac, Allen Ginsberg, and Lawrence Ferlinghetti were among the Beats who embraced this three-line, seventeen-syllable form of verse.

By then *bonsai* was also popular in the US, the pruning technique having been admired by American servicemen stationed in Japan in the 1940s, along with the paper technique of *origami*. These soldiers also brought home the word **honcho,** a near mirror image of the Japanese *hanchō* —originally used to describe military hotshots, now used to describe hotshots of all stripes.

But here's where the Japanese-English relationship gets really interesting. Ignoring the Shakespearean maxim of "neither a borrower nor a lender be," English has sometimes been both.

## 'Mind if I borrow that word back?'

"English seems to be quite eager to borrow back the words it lends to Japanese, usually after Japanese has done something interesting to them," observes Danica Salazar, the World English Editor of the *OED*.

As an example, Salazar explains how Japanese turned the English theatrical term "costume play" into *kosuchūmu-purē* first, then shortened it to *kosupure*. English borrowed it back as **cosplay.**

Are you a fan of **anime**? Sounds a lot like "animation," doesn't it? That's the word that English loaned and Japanese borrowed, Salazar says, as *animēshon*. Then English borrowed it back as anime.

More and more, though, English just borrows straight from the Japanese playbook. What do you think about using picture characters? If that sounds a bit bland, try the Japanese word instead: **emoji.**

## Wellspring Wonders

Now that you've had a tour of many of the languages packed into English, see if you can guess the etymology of these ten words. Choose the best of the three possibilities for each:

1. **skosh:** Swedish, Japanese, or Yiddish.
2. **boondocks:** German, Tagalog, or Gaelic.
3. **badlands:** Celtic, French, or Pennsylvania Dutch.

4. **jacaranda:** Spanish, Tupi, or Portuguese.
5. **ketchup:** Malay, Chinese, or Vietnamese.
6. **guano:** Nahuatl, Quechua, or Taíno.
7. **kumquat:** Japanese, Chinese, or Greek.
8. **bain-marie:** Danish, French, or Latin.
9. **jeroboam:** Gaelic, Hebrew, or Arabic.
10. **marzipan:** take your best guess.

As far as the answers, did you guess the pattern? It's the middle language for the first nine, with a few qualifiers here and there. We'll deal with marzipan later. Now for the stories.

**Skosh.** English ears may have an inclination to slide into *skoal*, the Scandinavian toasting equivalent of "cheers," when we hear this word. Not even close. Not even a skosh.

The word comes from the Japanese *sukoshi*, another that American servicemen stationed in Japan picked up. It means "a little" or "few." Its opposite, *takusan*, meaning "lots," never caught on with the Americans, as Kelly of Mashed Radish tells us. We'll just have to make do with a skosh.

**Boondocks.** The American military strikes again. This time in the Philippines, with the soldiers stationed there in the early 1900s. They took the Tagalog *bundok,* meaning "mountain," and turned it into "a remote, rough place." During World War II, soldiers stationed in such places wore combat, or field, boots that could handle rough terrain. They christened them **boondockers.**

**Badlands.** Talk about rough terrain. When French-Canadian trappers of the 1850s hit what is now the southwestern part of South Dakota, they described the area as *mauvaises terres pour traverser*—literally, "bad lands to traverse." English borrowed the *mauvaises terres* with its literal translation (known as a calque) and made the two words—bad lands—one.

**Jacaranda.** You still get points if you said this was Portuguese (it is: *jacarandá*), but it originated with the Native Tupi-Guaraní of South

America, who call this tree *yucaranda*. Some sources say the word translates to "fragrant," although the tree's blue-violet flowers have only a mild bouquet. Never mind—their color is exquisite.

**Ketchup.** If you chose Malay or Vietnamese for your answer, you'd still be in the ballpark. The history of the word is somewhat muddled, much like this condiment's ingredients. Both countries are mentioned in origin stories, but "ketchup" most likely comes from the Chinese *kê-chiap*, meaning "brine of fish."

The British were the first in Europe to catch on to this fish sauce, in the late 1600s. An English dictionary of the time spelled it "catchup." There was nary a tomato to be found in Britain's first versions; instead, cockles and mussels and beer and mushrooms were among the ingredients. The tomato version would, um, catch up in the early 1800s, in America. And then came Heinz, in 1876—not with "ketchup," but with the spelling Jonathan Swift favored in his 1730 poem, *A Panegyric on the Dean:* catsup.

**Guano.** The word in Quechua is *huanu*, meaning dung, and bird droppings in particular.

In the West Passage of Rhode Island's Narragansett Bay, Plum Beach Light's beacon still shines. But that's only because of a massive restoration project completed in 2003. Among other remediation measures, it removed the layers of guano that literally covered the 1899 lighthouse, outside and in. While it's no good for lighthouses, guano is very good for crops. It's an excellent fertilizer, as Stephen Moss relays in *Ten Birds That Changed the World*. The West cottoned onto this in the late 1800s, courtesy of the guanay cormorant in Peru (hence the Quechua connection). So much of this so-called brown gold was subsequently harvested that it threatened the bird's breeding ground. Using the guano as fertilizer, Moss says, "shaped the rural landscape of North America, Britain and much of the rest of Europe."

**Kumquat.** The fruit is native to southeast China, where its name translates to "gold tangerine." Its genus is not something we wordies usually fixate on, but this one—*Fortunella*—tells a good tale. It's named for Robert Fortune, the British botanist who first brought the fruit to

Europe in the 1860s. Fortune would subsequently make good on his name, when he returned to China to basically steal its secrets for making tea and brought them back to Britain.

**Bain-Marie.** This French term literally means "bath of Mary." (*Psst!* It's a double-boiler.) A Jewish woman named Marie who lived sometime between the first and third centuries in Alexandria, Egypt, invented this laboratory bath. She was one of the first recognized practitioners of alchemy and formulated a pigment in the desirable color of purple. The bain-marie was also desirable, as it resulted in a more uniform and safer way of heating that was just far enough away from the flame. If you've ever used a double-boiler, you know that the two-pot structure features water in the bottom pot—the one in contact with the heating element—and the material to be heated nested in the pot above it.

**Jeroboam.** The word derives from the Hebrew name for the ancient Israeli king *Yarobh'am*. Today it's a description for a large bottle of wine, one holding between three and four-and-a-half liters. (A standard-size bottle holds 750 milliliters.) For a somewhat princely sum, you'll enjoy twenty-four glasses or more of wine.

Even with wine, size matters: a larger bottle is said to deliver a better-aged wine. And while the jeroboam is big, other bottles are bigger. Many of these also have Biblical names. There's the six-liter Methuselah, which summons the name of the Old Testament's oldest person—north of nine hundred years and the grandfather of Noah. Then there's the twelve-liter Balthazar, with the name of one of the three wise men, or Magi. And with the eighteen-liter Solomon, we come full circle to the name of another king of Israel, this one known for his wisdom.

Okay, but why Biblical names for imbibing?

"My sense is this: Somebody, whoever came up with these conventions—we really don't know—wanted to give wine a kind of royal or aristocratic association," says Rod Phillips, a wine historian who also teaches the history of food and alcohol at Carleton University in Ottawa, Canada. In this 2024 interview with the Jewish newspaper *Forward,* he added: "If you say Napoleon you upset the Brits. And if you say Churchill, you upset the French. And if you say Lincoln, people think of a car. So you go back to the bible."

## Now, About That Marzipan

If you savor the taste of this sweet, almondy confection, you know why a simple pleasure can seem sublime. The word's origin story, however, is anything but simple.

It could be German (*Marzipan*) or Italian (*marzapane*). Or Spanish (*mazapán*). In fact, as Pamela Vachon, a graduate of the Institute of Culinary Education, tells us, all three countries, along with Portugal, have areas that claim ownership.

Then again, the word might be Dutch or French. When all else fails, default to Latin. *Martius panis* means "bread of Mars," as in the Roman god of Mars, from which we derive our month of March, and from which Saint Mark derived his name—so it's sometimes translated as "bread of Mark."

One story goes that bread bakers in Italy turned to almonds when the wheat they normally used was scarce. The sweet taste was a hit and the bakers segued to making marzipan.

The anglicized version of *martius panis* became **marchpane,** a dessert that Shakespeare baked into his *Romeo and Juliet*, where a servant exhorts another to "save me a piece of marchpane."

*Okay great,* you say, *all's well that ends well.* Nope—not done yet.

"One suggestion," write the editors of the *Online Etymology Dictionary*, "is that this is from Arabic *mawthaban* 'king who sits still.' Nobody seems to quite accept this, but nobody has a better idea."

But that might not be such a bad idea, after all. An *Al-Andulus* newsletter of AramcoWorld relays how, in the city of Toledo on the Iberian peninsula, before marzipan was baked, a coin was pressed into the paste that featured a king on his throne (thus sitting still). "There was in fact a Byzantine coin, widely circulated in the Middle East by the year 1000, that showed a seated figure on the reverse, and which the Arabs called *mawthaban*."

Still not done.

In *The Secret Life of Words,* Henry Hitchings suggests the word "may have taken its name from a Burmese city known for its handsome storage jars." That would be the port of Martaban in what is now Myanmar, "once famous for the glazed jars it exported," Oxford Reference tells us, "containing preserves and sweets."

Okay, now we're done. Whew!

What's so delicious about marzipan (besides its taste, if you're a fan) is how the, shall we say, "uncertain origin" of the word takes us on the kind of etymological adventure that makes English so enticing.

Sweet.

# LAST WORDS (FOR NOW)

## 19.
## BILENGLISH, OR: WHAT LANGUAGE CAN YOU SPEAK WHEN YOU SPEAK ENGLISH?

Not that long ago a very smart person I know, who is also a gifted writer, told me they found reading about word origins "a real slog." And yet they had once delighted in relaying their discovery of where that cliché of a name for a dog, Fido, came from.

Perhaps there are more meanderthals in our midst than some of us realize.

(As for Fido—there's a reason my husband and I have never entertained the name for our miniature dachshunds. Fido comes from *fidelis*, which we saw in chapter 5 means faithful, suggesting some degree of obedience. As if.)

The historian David McCullough was fond of pointing out that if we don't know where we've come from, we don't really know who we are. For native-English speakers, knowing more about where our language has come from can help us better appreciate all the languages that went into what it's become. And appreciate languages, period.

But let's face it, for many of us, trying to learn one of those other languages as an adult can be a real slog at times. So if our meanderthalling ways and penchant for knowing some of the history behind the words can help, *tant mieux:* so much the better. Just like foodies, we wordies want to know the ingredients—in essence, the stories that etymologies hold. And sometimes there's more than one.

## 'There's a story behind this'

In his book *Learn Spanish via Etymologies,* S. Morgan Friedman shares tales and tips that help decode English translations of certain Spanish words. One of just many examples he gives is *hablar,* meaning to speak or talk. He unspools the Spanish to the Latin *fabulare,* meaning to talk or tell a story, from which we get **fable**. He then shows us a pattern: "as Latin evolved into Spanish," he explains, "the letter 'F' followed by a vowel became an 'H.'"

Then there's *faro,* which is Spanish for lighthouse. There's surely no kissin'-cousin cognate there, but there's a great story from whence it came. On a small island called Pharos in the harbor of ancient Alexandria in Egypt, there stood the world's first lighthouse, as dazzling as Alexandria's famous library. In those days of grandeur, writes Islam Issa in his cultural history of the city, "Alexandria was something of a New York, the Pharos Lighthouse its Lady Liberty." For much of that part of the world, the name Pharos became synonymous with lighthouse. Knowing this story, you're likely to remember what *faro* means in Spanish, or *phare* in French, or *faro* in Italian or Galician, or *farol* in Portuguese, or *far* in Romanian.

One more: the Spanish *cura,* which translates to "cure," comes from the Latin for "care." *And your point,* you're probably yawning. It's this: *cura* in Spanish also means "priest," described in *Elsevier's Concise Spanish Etymological Dictionary* as "one who takes care of souls." And while we now use "curate," another derivative, as a verb, in liturgical circles the noun **curate** describes a parish priest.

Once you become a seeker of stories while learning another language, you might also start sussing out patterns—for example, if *ver* in Spanish means to see, then *prever* must mean to "pre-see"—to foresee, in other words.

Of course, Spanish and French and Italian (and more) being Romance languages, and English vocabulary being besotted with Romance words, makes all this easier than, say, trying to learn Arabic. Even so, Arabic has a root system consisting of three letters that can help native-English speakers see patterns.

As the Arab Academy tells us, "Every word with the same three root letters can be categorized into similar areas." As an example, the Academy uses the three root letters of k, t, and b, which are connected to writing. So while we may not immediately know what *kitaab* and *maktab* mean, we at least know that both have something to do with writing. *Kitaab*, the Academy tells us, means book. *Maktab* means desk or office. So from there, we're not surprised to learn that *maktaba* means library. How cool is this—and we think so because we're language lovers. I mean really, what's not to love?

And it's not like we need different parts of our brain to learn different languages, even if they are far distant from our own. "The brain does not process each language in one specific area," the psycholinguist and cognitive scientist Viorica Marian assures us. "Instead, a broad and highly interconnected and distributed neural network is used both within and across languages."

## Besides, if you're older, you're smarter

And all along you've been thinking that as an adult, you were merely wiser. But your "crystallized" intelligence is stronger than you may realize, especially if you rightly suspect that your "fluid" intelligence is weakening as you get older.

"Fluid intelligence involves the ability to reason and think flexibly, whereas crystallized intelligence refers to the accumulation of knowledge, facts, and skills acquired throughout life," explains psychologist Kendry Cherry, author of *The Everything Psychology Book*.

So even though you may not feel so smart when, for example, you try to master a new video game having never played one, you're smarter than you may think when it comes to learning a new language. The video game taps into "fluid" intelligence, while tackling a new language taps into "crystallized" intelligence. You're basically applying all that accumulated knowledge you have about the English language to the language you're learning. Vocabulary and grammar in particular come into play here.

So let's hear it for the word lovers. Because it seems to follow that the more we know about how so many words in the English language started off in another language, the more our "crystallized" intelligence can kick in.

## Going all in

As you might guess from his name, Mohamed Kilani, a 2021 graduate of Bowdoin College, is Arab, from Jordan. While his first language is Arabic, he also speaks French and is fluent in English and Spanish. He teaches the latter to elementary school students in Maine. "I think it's easy for someone speaking Arabic to learn Spanish," he says of his career choice. A one-time refugee in the US with his mother and brother, Mohamed and his family are now American citizens.

He sees language learning as "an empathetic thing you can do for someone else." He knows how much it means to newcomers if we learn even just "a few phrases," as he says, of their native language.

His use of the word "empathetic" is telling. **Empathy** is a word Greek has had for ages, but not so English. It's been part of the English lexicon for only about a century, and not from Greek but from the German *Einfühlung*: literally "in-feeling."

Learning another's language is often considered a way to up one's empathy meter. As Viorica Marian observes, "Simply the awareness that the language or culture of the person you are interacting with may be different from yours can shift social dynamics."

Even if going all in on learning another language is not right for you right now, going all in on appreciating other languages—perhaps even learning a few of those phrases—may well be. And not in spite of English, but because of it. As the writer and linguist Ilan Stavans, an American by way of Mexico, observes: "From the start, this nation's language has existed in a state of constant innovation."

While some see the English language as a roadblock to learning other languages, we wordies think it quite the opposite because of its rich, multilingual history that we live every time we speak it. This is where we come from (with a nod to David McCullough), and this is who we are.

So never mind that roadblock—go for the open road, knowing that sometimes the best way to come to another language is to start by relishing your own. It's got a heck of a story to tell.

I wish you good meanderthalling. And no, that word is not in the dictionary.

At least, not yet.

～～～～

*"You can never understand one language until you understand at least two."*
— Marcus Fabius Quintilian

# BIBLIOGRAPHY

**PRINT**

Achenbach, Joel. *The Grand Idea: George Washington's Potomac and the Race to the West.* New York: Simon & Schuster, 2004.

Allman, T.D. *Finding Florida: The True History of the Sunshine State.* New York: Grove Press, 2013.

Atwell, Mary Stewart. "Hallowed Land: Preserving South Carolina's Gullah Culture." *The New York Times*, April 21, 2019.

Aurelius, Marcus. *Shirt Pocket Wisdom: Marcus Aurelius's* Meditations. Delray Beach, FL: Levenger Press, 2014.

Barnett, Cynthia. *The Sound of the Sea: Seashells and the Fate of the Oceans.* New York: W.W. Norton & Company, 2021.

Barton, Polly. *Fifty Sounds: A Memoir of Language, Learning, and Longing.* New York: Liveright Publishing, 2022.

Bauer, Laurie. *The Linguistics Student's Handbook.* New York: Oxford University Press, 2007.

Baugh, Albert C., and Thomas Cable. *A History of the English Language.* 6th ed. Abingdon, UK: Routledge, 2012.

Berman, Eleanor Davidson. *Thomas Jefferson Among the Arts.* New York: Philosophical Library, 1947.

Berry, Jessica. *The Little Gullah Geechee Book.* Orangeburg, SC: J. Berry Collective, LLC, 2020.

# BIBLIOGRAPHY

Boshoff, Jaco Jacques, Lonnie G. Bunch III, Paul Gardullo, and Stephen C. Lubkemann. *From No Return: The 221-Year Journey of the Slave Ship São José.* Washington, DC: Smithsonian Enterprises, on behalf of the Smithsonian Institution and the National Museum of African American History and Culture, 2016.

Brady, Michael Patrick. "The Talk of Ancient Riders": Review of *Proto*, by Laura Spinney. *The Wall Street Journal,* May 10–11, 2025.

Bragg, Melvyn. *The Adventure of English.* London: Hodder & Stoughton, 2004.

Bridgeford, Andrew. *1066: The Hidden History in the Bayeux Tapestry.* New York: Walker & Company, 2005.

Brown, Alphonso. *A Gullah Guide to Charleston.* Charleston, SC: The History Press, 2008.

Brown, Patricia Leigh. "Show of Strength for Preservation of Praise Houses." *The New York Times,* November 26, 2023.

Cassidy, Cody. *Who Ate the First Oyster? The Extraordinary People Behind the Greatest Firsts in History.* New York: Penguin, 2020.

Cawdrey, Robert. *The First English Dictionary, 1604.* Oxford: Bodleian Library, 2007.

Chan, Phil. "My Porcelain Sickness." In Meredith Martin, ed., *Reimagining the* Ballet des Porcelaines: *A Tale of Magic, Desire, and Exotic Entanglement,* 54–69. Turnhout, Belgium: Harvey Miller Publishers, 2022.

Chant, Joy. *The High Kings: Arthur's Celtic Ancestors.* Toronto and New York: Bantam Books, 1983.

Cook, Vivian. *Accommodating Brocolli in the Cemetary: or Why Can't Anybody Spell?* New York: Touchstone, 2005.

Cross, Wilbur, and Eric Crawford. *Gullah Culture in America.* 2nd ed. Durham, NC: Blair, 2023.

Crystal, David. *Spell It Out: The Curious, Enthralling and Extraordinary Story of English Spelling.* New York: St. Martin's Press, 2013.

Crystal, David, and Ben Crystal. *The Shakespeare Miscellany.* New York: The Overlook Press, 2005.

Curzan, Anne. *Gender Shifts in the History of English.* Cambridge: Cambridge University Press, 2003.

Dalrymple, William. *The Anarchy: The East India Company, Corporate Violence, and the Pillage of an Empire.* New York: Bloomsbury, 2019.

Delahunty, Andrew, Sheila Dignen, and Penny Stock. *The Oxford Dictionary of Allusions.* Oxford and New York: Oxford University Press, 2001.

# BIBLIOGRAPHY

Doerr, Anthony. *Cloud Cuckoo Land.* New York: Scribner, 2021.

Dorren, Gaston. *Babel: Around the World in Twenty Languages.* New York: Atlantic Monthly Press, 2018.

Dunn, Jon. *The Glitter in the Green: In Search of Hummingbirds.* New York: Basic Books, 2021.

Ehrenberg, Ralph E., and Herman J. Viola. *Mapping the West with Lewis and Clark.* Delray Beach, FL: Levenger Press, 2015.

Fabricant, Florence. "Underrated Fish Wins New Fans." *The New York Times*, August 25, 2021.

Ferguson, Georgie V. "We Are Pointe Au Chien." In *French All Around Us: French Language and Francophone Culture in the United States*, edited by Kathleen Stein-Smith and Fabrice Jaumont, 97–106. New York and Paris: TBR Books, 2022.

Flanders, Judith. *A Place for Everything: The Curious History of Alphabetical Order.* New York: Basic Books, 2020.

Flournoy, Angela. "Our Rice, Ourselves." *The New York Times Magazine*, November 14, 2021.

Friedman, S. Morgan. *Learn Spanish via Etymologies.* Self-published, 2018.

Geraty, Virginia Mixson. *Gulluh Fuh Oonuh (Gullah for You): A Guide to the Gullah Language.* Orangeburg, SC: Sandlapper Publishing, 1997.

Gleick, James. *The Information: A History, A Theory, A Flood.* New York: Pantheon Books, 2011.

Gordon, James D. *The English Language: An Historical Introduction.* New York: Thomas Y. Crowell Company, 1972.

Green, Dominic. "Seeking Illumination": Review of *The Manuscripts Club*, by Christopher de Hamel. *The Wall Street Journal*, November 18–19, 2023.

Green, Matthew. *Shadowlands: A Journey Through Britain's Lost Cities and Vanished Villages.* New York: W.W. Norton & Company, 2022.

Hansen, Valerie. *The Year 1000: When Explorers Connected the World—and Globalization Began.* New York: Scribner, 2020.

Harris, Elizabeth A. "A New Lexicon That Is Proudly African American." *The New York Times*, July 22, 2022.

Herman, Arthur. *The Viking Heart: How Scandinavians Conquered the World.* New York: Houghton Mifflin Harcourt, 2021.

Hessler, John W., and Chet Van Duzer. *Seeing the World Anew: The Radical Vision of Martin Waldseemüller's 1507 & 1516 World Maps.* Delray Beach, FL: Levenger Press, 2012.

# BIBLIOGRAPHY

Hitchings, Henry. *The Secret Life of Words: How English Became English.* New York: Farrar, Straus and Giroux, 2008.

Hoad, T.F., ed. *The Concise Oxford Dictionary of English Etymology.* Oxford and New York: Oxford University Press, 2003.

Immerwahr, Daniel. "Change the Map, Change the Moral." *The Atlantic*, May 2022.

Indian Pueblo Cultural Center. *Gateway to the 19 Pueblos of New Mexico.* Albuquerque, NM. Exhibition catalog.

Issa, Islam. *Alexandria: The City That Changed the World.* New York: Pegasus Books, 2024.

Jarman, Cat. *River Kings: A New History of the Vikings from Scandinavia to the Silk Roads.* New York: Pegasus Books, 2022.

Jelly-Schapiro, Joshua. *Names of New York: Discovering the City's Past, Present, and Future Through Its Place-Names.* New York: Pantheon, 2021.

Judge, Gary. *The Timeline History of the English Language.* Yokohama, Japan: Cogno Graphica Publishing, 2010.

Katz, Josh. *Speaking American: How Y'all, Youse, and You Guys Talk—A Visual Guide.* New York: Mariner Books, 2020.

Kennedy, John F. *The Making of His Inaugural Address.* Delray Beach, FL: Levenger Press, 2009.

King, Ross. *The Bookseller of Florence: The Story of the Manuscripts That Illuminated the Renaissance.* New York: Atlantic Monthly Press, 2021.

Koenig, John. *The Dictionary of Obscure Sorrows.* New York: Simon & Schuster, 2021.

Koerner, Brendan I. "The Hibernator's Guide to the Galaxy." *Wired* Magazine, December 2022–January 2023.

Labine, Mark. "French Heritage in Minnesota." In Stein-Smith and Jaumont, eds., *French All Around Us*, 122–31.

Lepore, Jill. "Noah's Mark: Webster and the Original Dictionary Wars." *The New Yorker*, November 6, 2006.

Lester, Toby. *The Fourth Part of the World: The Race to the Ends of the Earth, and the Epic Story of the Map That Gave America Its Name.* New York: Free Press, 2009.

Leveen, Steve. *America's Bilingual Century: How Americans Are Giving the Gift of Bilingualism to Themselves, Their Loved Ones, and Their Country.* Delray Beach, FL: America the Bilingual Press, 2021.

# BIBLIOGRAPHY

Liberman, Anatoly. *Word Origins: And How We Know Them.* New York: Oxford University Press, 2005.

Lidz, Franz. "Unearthing a Maya Civilization That 'Punched Above Its Weight.'" *The New York Times*, September 13, 2022.

Lumsden, Roddy. *Vitamin Q: A Temple of Trivia Lists and Curious Words.* Edinburgh: Chambers Harrap Publishers, 2004.

Lynch, Jack. *The Lexicographer's Dilemma.* New York: Walker Publishing, 2009.

Lynch, Jack, ed. *Samuel Johnson's Dictionary: Selections from the 1755 Work That Defined the English Language.* Delray Beach, FL: Levenger Press, 2002.

Mack, Stephen. *It Had to Be Done: The Navajo Code Talkers Remember World War II.* Marana, AZ: Whispering Dove Design, 2008.

Magennis, Hugh. *Translating Beowulf: Modern Verses in English Verse.* Woodbridge, UK: D.S. Brewer, 2011.

Marian, Viorica. *The Power of Language: How the Codes We Use to Think, Speak, and Live Transform Our Minds.* New York: Dutton, 2023.

Martineau, Jesse, and Monique Cairns. "French Language and Francophone Culture in New England and the French-Canadian Legacy Podcast and Blog." In Stein-Smith and Jaumont, eds., *French All Around Us*, 181–93.

McCrum, Robert, William Cran, and Robert MacNeil. *The Story of English.* New York: Elizabeth Sifton Books/Viking, 1986.

McQuain, Jeffrey, and Stanley Malless. *Coined by Shakespeare.* Springfield, MA: Merriam-Webster, 1998.

McWhorter, John H. *The Missing Spanish Creoles: Recovering the Birth of Plantation Contact.* Oakland, CA: University of California Press, 2000.

—. *Myths, Lies, and Half-Truths of Language Usage: Course Guidebook.* Chantilly, VA: The Great Courses, 2012.

—. *Talking Back, Talking Black: Truths About America's Lingua Franca.* New York: Bellevue Literary Press, 2017.

Méheut, Constant. "Beloved Bookstores Fold, and an Enclave's Spirit Dims." *The New York Times,* March 24, 2021.

*Merriam-Webster's Encyclopedia of Literature.* Springfield, MA: Merriam-Webster, 1995, s.v.v. "Lothario," "Quixote."

*Merriam-Webster's Spanish-English Dictionary.* Springfield, MA: Merriam-Webster, 2014.

More, Thomas. *Libellus vere aureus nec Minus Salutaris Quam Festivus de optimo reip. statu, deq; nova Insula Utopia.* Louvain: Arte Theodorici Martini, 1516.

# BIBLIOGRAPHY

Henry W. and Albert A. Berg Collection of English and American Literature, The New York Public Library.

Morley, Simon. *By Any Other Name: A Cultural History of the Rose.* London: Oneworld Publications, 2021. As cited in David Propson, "The Queen of Flowers," *The Wall Street Journal*, February 12–13, 2022.

Morris, John Miller, ed. *Narrative of the Coronado Expedition by Pedro de Castañeda de Nájera,* 1540–42. Translated from the Spanish by George P. Hammond and Agapito Rey. Chicago: R.R. Donnelley & Sons Company, The Lakeside Press, 2002.

Moss, Stephen. *Ten Birds That Changed the World.* New York: Basic Books, 2023.

Mufwene, Salikoko S. "The Emergence of African American English: Monogenetic or Polygenetic? With or Without 'Decreolization'? Under How Much Substrate Influence?" In Sonja Lanehart, ed., *The Oxford Handbook of African American Language,* 57–84. New York: Oxford University Press, 2015.

Norris, Mary. *Greek to Me: Adventures of the Comma Queen.* New York: W.W. Norton & Company, 2019.

O'Conner, Patricia T., and Stewart Kellerman. *Origins of the Specious: Myths and Misconceptions of the English Language.* New York: Random House, 2010.

Onishi, Norimitsu. "A Conciliatory Gesture, or Just an Empty Gift?" *The New York Times,* May 28, 2023.

Ostler, Rosemarie. *The United States of English: The American Language from Colonial Times to the Twenty-First Century.* New York: Oxford University Press, 2023.

*Oxford English Dictionary.* 2nd ed. Vol. I. Oxford: Clarendon Press, 1989, s.v. "aficionado."

—. Vol. III. Oxford: Clarendon Press, 1989, s.v. "colonize."

—. Vol. XI. Oxford: Clarendon Press, 1989, s.v. "penguin."

—. Vol. XIII. Oxford: Clarendon Press, 1989, s.v. "quixotic."

—. Vol. XVII. Oxford: Clarendon Press, 1989, s.v. "superstition."

Pané, Fray Ramón. *An Account of the Antiquities of the Indians.* Edited by José Juan Arrom. Translated by Susan C. Griswald. Durham, NC: Duke University Press, 1999.

Paulson, Scott. *English and Spanish: The Similarities and Differences.* Self-published, 2019.

Pearson, Barry Lee. *Jook Right On: Blues Stories and Blues Storytellers.* Knoxville: University of Tennessee Press, 2005.

Perlin, Ross. *Language City: The Fight to Preserve Endangered Mother Tongues in New York.* New York: Atlantic Monthly Press, 2024.

# BIBLIOGRAPHY

Preston, Diana and Michael. *A Pirate of Exquisite Mind. Explorer, Naturalist, and Buccaneer: The Life of William Dampier.* New York: Walker & Company, 2004.

Pyles, Thomas, and John Algeo. *The Origins and Development of the English Language.* 3rd ed. New York: Harcourt Brace Jovanovich, 1982.

Rogers, Susan, and Ogi Ogas. *This Is What It Sounds Like: What the Music You Love Says About You.* New York: W.W. Norton & Company, 2022.

Roosevelt, Theodore. *New York.* Delray Beach, FL: Levenger Press, 2004. Abridged edition of the 1891 original published by Longmans, Green, and Co.

Salam, Maya. "Private Parts": Review of *Vagina Obscura: An Anatomical Voyage,* by Rachel E. Gross. *The New York Times Book Review,* April 10, 2022.

Schiff, Stacy. *The Revolutionary: Samuel Adams.* New York: Little, Brown and Company, 2022.

Sequoyah. *Cherokee syllabary.* Cherokee Baptist Mission Press: H. Upham, Printer, ca. 1845. Rare Book Division, The New York Public Library.

Specia, Megan. "An Ancient Tongue Heard Even in the Children's Chatter." *The New York Times,* November 25, 2022.

Stamper, Kory. *Word by Word: The Secret Life of Dictionaries.* New York: Vintage Books, 2018.

Stavans, Ilan. "How We the People Built American English." *The Wall Street Journal,* March 4–5, 2023.

Stein-Smith, Kathleen, and Fabrice Jaumont, eds., *French All Around Us: French Language and Francophone Culture in the United States.* New York and Paris: TBR Books, 2022.

Talbot, Margaret. "Starting Fresh." *The New Yorker,* January 18, 2021.

Tiro, Karim M. *Words & Deeds: Natives, Europeans, and Writing in Eastern North America, 1500–1850.* Philadelphia: The Rosenbach Museum & Library, 1997. Exhibition catalog.

Tocqueville, Alexis de. *A Fortnight in the Wilderness.* Translated by George Lawrence. Delray Beach, FL: Levenger Press, 2003.

Unger, Harlow Giles. *Noah Webster: The Life and Times of an American Patriot.* New York: John Wiley & Sons, 1998.

Van Duzer, Chet, John W. Hessler, and Daniel De Simone. *Christopher Columbus Book of Privileges: The Claiming of a New World, 1502.* Delray Beach, FL: Levenger Press, 2014.

Varadarajan, Tunku. "Empire and Its Aftermath": Review of *España: A Brief History of Spain,* by Giles Tremlett. *The Wall Street Journal,* October 8–9, 2022.

# BIBLIOGRAPHY

Vignon, Charlotte. "Conjuring 1740: A Tale of Europe's Obsession with Porcelain." In Martin, ed., *Reimagining the* Ballet des Porcelaines, 70–87.

Watson, Cecilia. *Semicolon: The Past, Present, and Future of a Misunderstood Mark.* New York: HarperCollins, 2019.

Weldon, Tracey L., and Simanique Moody. "The Place of Gullah in the African American Linguistic Continuum." In Lanehart, ed., *The Oxford Handbook of African American Language*, 163–80.

White, R.J. *The Horizon Concise History of England.* New York: American Heritage Publishing Co., 1971.

Williams, Pip. *The Dictionary of Lost Words.* New York: Ballantine Books, 2022.

Winford, Donald. "The Origins of African American Vernacular English: Beginnings." In Lanehart, ed., *The Oxford Handbook of African American Language*, 85–104.

Wright, Alex. *Glut: Mastering Information Through the Ages.* Washington, DC: Joseph Henry Press, 2007.

Yezzi, David. "The Banjo's Resonant Story": Review of *Well of Souls*, by Kristina R. Gaddy. *The Wall Street Journal,* November 12–13, 2022.

Zimmer, Ben. "An Ancient Name for a Stormy Sea-Born Threat." *The Wall Street Journal,* November 21–22, 2020.

—. "Spreading the Faith, in Religion or Politics." *The Wall Street Journal,* April 9–10, 2022.

## ELECTRONIC
**The Indispensables**
Many individual websites provided the first look at words to see if their history would be enticing to word lovers. The sources listed immediately below provided amplification, corroboration, and where needed, corrections.

*Britannica* encyclopedia. https://www.britannica.com.

*Cambridge Dictionary.* https://dictionary.cambridge.org/us/dictionary/english/.

*Collins English Dictionary.* https://www.collinsdictionary.com/us/.

*Collins English Dictionary: Language Lover* blog. https://blog.collinsdictionary.com/tag/word-origins/.

*Merriam-Webster* dictionary. https://www.merriam-webster.com/.

*Online Etymology Dictionary.* https://www.etymonline.com/.

SpanishDictionary.com. https://www.spanishdict.com/.

Vocabulary.com. https://www.vocabulary.com/.

# BIBLIOGRAPHY

ACTFL. "Cognates." *Glossary*. https://www.actfl.org/educator-resources/actfl-proficiency-guidelines/glossary.

Acutrans. "Top 10 Languages of Louisiana." May 17, 2023. https://acutrans.com/top-10-languages-of-louisiana/.

African American Registry. "The Banjo's African, and African American Heritage: A Story." https://aaregistry.org/story/the-banjos-african-american-heritage/.

Agan, Kelly, Steven Case, and Amy Kemp. "State Fruit of North Carolina: Scuppernong Grape." NCpedia, an online encyclopedia of North Carolina. https://www.ncpedia.org/symbols/fruit.

Alexpolistigers. "Swellings and Seals: On the Origins of Bill." *Glossologics* blog, November 25, 2016. https://alexpolistigers.wordpress.com/2016/11/25/swellings-and-seals-on-the-origins-of-bill/.

Alkazwini, Azhar A. "The Linguistic Influence of the Norman Conquest (11th Century) on the English Language." *International Journal of Linguistics* 8, no. 3 (2016). doi: 10.5296/ijl.v8i3.9526.

Allen, Erin. "See It Now: *Columbus's Book of Privileges*." Library of Congress blog, October 13, 2014. https://blogs.loc.gov/loc/2014/10/see-it-now-columbuss-book-of-privileges/. See embedded video.

America the Bilingual. "Africa's Relaxed Multilingualism." *America the Bilingual* (podcast). Episode 44, 2019. https://www.americathebilingual.com/44-africas-relaxed-multilingualism/.

—. "Chef Pati Jinich's Recipe for Reaching Across Cultures." *America the Bilingual* (podcast). Episode 63, 2023. https://www.americathebilingual.com/63-chef-pati-jinichs-recipe-for-reaching-across-cultures/.

—. "In Case You Thought Latin Was Dead . . . ." *America the Bilingual* (podcast). Episode 23, 2018. https://www.americathebilingual.com/in-case-you-thought-latin-was-dead/.

—. "Meet a Spanish Teacher in Maine Named Mohamed." *America the Bilingual* (podcast). Episode 67, 2023. https://www.americathebilingual.com/67-meet-a-spanish-teacher-in-maine-named-mohamed/.

—. "Reclaiming the Language That History Wanted Lost." *America the Bilingual* (podcast). Episode 58, 2023. https://www.americathebilingual.com/58-reclaiming-the-language-that-history-wanted-lost/.

# BIBLIOGRAPHY

Anacostia Community Museum. "'Word, Shout, Song: Lorenzo Dow Turner Connecting Communities through Language' Opens at the Anacostia Community Museum." Smithsonian Institution news release, August 4, 2010. https://www.si.edu/newsdesk/releases/word-shout-song-lorenzo-dow-turner-connecting-communities-through-language-opens-anacostia-.

Anastopoulo, Rossi. "What Is Pâte à Choux? Why We Love This Versatile French Dough." King Arthur Baking Company blog, October 24, 2022. https://www.kingarthurbaking.com/blog/2022/10/24/what-is-pate-a-choux-why-we-love-this-versatile-french-dough.

Anderson, Emma. "20 Cool German Words." *Foreign Language Immersion Online* blog. FluentU, August 14, 2024. https://www.fluentu.com/blog/german/cool-german-words/.

Andreu, Michael G., Melissa H. Friedman, and Robert J. Northrop. "*Fortunella* spp., Kumquat." University of Florida, Institute of Food and Agricultural Sciences Extension Service. https://edis.ifas.ufl.edu/publication/FR368.

Andrews, Evan. "America's Forgotten Swedish Colony." History, August 23, 2018. https://www.history.com/news/americas-forgotten-swedish-colony.

Anonymous. *Beowulf* (Old English version). The Poetry Foundation. https://www.poetryfoundation.org/poems/43521/beowulf-old-english-version.

Arab Academy. "English Words That Come From Arabic." July 19, 2017. https://www.arabacademy.com/english-words-come-arabic/.

—. "Surprising Facts about the Arabic Language." March 15, 2017. https://www.arabacademy.com/surprising-facts-arabic-language/.

Arabic for Beginners. "Arabic Root System Overview" lesson. https://arabicforbeginners.com/topic/arabic-root-system-overview/.

Bailey, Guy. "The History of African-American Vernacular English." In *Oxford Research Encyclopedia of Linguistics* (online). Oxford University Press: August 15, 2022. https://doi.org/10.1093/acrefore/9780199384655.013.926.

Barr, Andrew. "If You're Over 40 and Learning Spanish, Watch This." RealFastSpanish.com YouTube video. N.d. https://www.youtube.com/watch?v=wIaPDassnQw.

—. "1001 Spanish Words You Already Know—A Guide To English-Spanish Cognates." RealFastSpanish.com. https://www.realfastspanish.com/vocabulary/spanish-cognates.

BBC Cymru. "Geoffrey of Monmouth." *Wales History*, 2014. https://www.bbc.co.uk/wales/history/sites/themes/figures/geoffrey_of_monmouth.shtml.

# BIBLIOGRAPHY

BBC News. "How the Ancient Welsh Language Helped Shape English," December 1, 2010. https://www.bbc.com/news/uk-wales-11887312.

—. "Manx Gaelic 'Not Extinct' Says UN," August 19, 2009. http://news.bbc.co.uk/2/hi/europe/isle_of_man/8210192.stm.

—. "Record Number of Cornish Choughs Fledge," August 3, 2021. https://www.bbc.com/news/uk-england-cornwall-58070518.

BBC Online. "Christianity in Britain." April 27, 2011. https://www.bbc.co.uk/religion/religions/christianity/history/uk_1.shtml.

—. "Languages Across Europe." October 14, 2014. https://www.bbc.co.uk/languages/european_languages/languages/greek.shtml.

BCN Exclusive Private Tours. "A Brief History of the Spanish Siesta" blog. https://barcelonaexclusiveprivatetours.com/blog/a-brief-history-of-the-spanish-siesta.

Beale, Stephen. "12 Latin Words That Shaped the Faith." Catholic Exchange, February 24, 2014. https://catholicexchange.com/12-latin-words-shaped-faith/.

Becchi, Michela. "Marzipan: History, Recipes and Variations of the Typical Sweet Pastry of Sicily." Gambero Rosso, March 30, 2021. https://www.gamberorossointernational.com/news/food-news/marzipan-history-recipes-and-variations-of-the-typical-sweet-pastry-of-sicily/.

Belinsky, Natalya. "Everyday Yiddish-English-Yiddish Dictionary." TranslationDirectory.com. https://www.translationdirectory.com/dictionaries/dictionary004_s.htm.

Betts, Jennifer. "Fearless Norse Words Found in Everyday English." YourDictionary. https://grammar.yourdictionary.com/word-lists/fearless-norse-words-found-everyday-english.

Beverley Minster website. "Sanctuary Crosses." https://beverleyminster.org.uk/sanctuary/sanctuary-crosses/.

Biography.com editors. "Saint Patrick Biography." A&E Television Networks: Biography website, April 20, 2021. https://www.biography.com/religious-figure/saint-patrick.

Blackburn, Jim. "Was the Early Church 'Catholic' or Just 'Christian'?" *Catholic Answers*, April 1, 2019. https://www.catholic.com/magazine/online-edition/was-the-early-church-catholic-or-just-christian.

Bluetooth. "Origin of the Bluetooth Name." Bluetooth website. https://www.bluetooth.com/about-us/bluetooth-origin/.

# BIBLIOGRAPHY

Boston University. "Virginia Woolf on Not Knowing Greek." *The Core Blog*, July 19, 2018. https://blogs.bu.edu/core/2018/07/19/virginia-woolf-on-not-knowing-greek/.

Bouchard, R. Philip. "Breakfast, Lunch & Dinner." *Word Connections* blog, January 10, 2017. https://medium.com/the-philipendium/word-connections-breakfast-lunch-dinner-2e5d06c79bac.

British Library. "Lindisfarne Gospels." https://www.bl.uk/collection-items/lindisfarne-gospels.

—. "*The Recuyell of the Historyes of Troye*." https://www.bl.uk/collection-items/the-recuyell-of-the-historyes-of-troye.

Brouwers, Josho. "Troilus and Cressida: A Medieval Love Story." *Ancient World* online magazine, November 12, 2021. https://www.ancientworldmagazine.com/articles/troilus-cressida.

Campbell, Lyle, and William O. Bright. "North American Indian Languages." *Encyclopedia Britannica*, July 14, 2016. https://www.britannica.com/topic/North-American-Indian-languages.

Carpenter, Wm. H. "Dutch Contributions to the Vocabulary of English in America: Dutch Remainders in New York State." *Modern Philology* 6, no. 1 (July 1908): 53–68. https://www.jstor.org/stable/432522.

Carter, Abi. "German Words Expats Should Know: Gemütlichkeit." Iam-Expat Media, November 3, 2023. https://www.iamexpat.de/education/education-news/german-words-expats-should-know-gemuetlichkeit.

Cartwright, Mark. "Wolof Empire." In *World History Encyclopedia*, November 20, 2019. https://www.worldhistory.org/Wolof_Empire/.

Casa Areyto. "Let's Talk Taíno 1—About Taíno Language." YouTube video, March 19, 2021. https://www.youtube.com/watch?v=nyox4qVTukg.

*Catholic Encyclopedia*, s.v. "aumbry." New York: Robert Appleton Company, 1907. http://www.newadvent.org/cathen/02107b.htm.

Central Intelligence Agency. "Navajo Code Talkers and the Unbreakable Code." Central Intelligence Agency Stories. November 6, 2008. https://www.cia.gov/stories/story/navajo-code-talkers-and-the-unbreakable-code/.

Charleston Footprints. "It Ain't Haint or Haint Blue" blog, July 25, 2012. https://www.charlestonfootprints.com/charleston-blog/it-aint-haint-or-haint-blue/2012/07/05/.

Château de Berne. "Size of wine bottles: Magnum, Jeroboam, Mathusalem ... " https://chateauberne-vin.com/en-be/blogs/news/taille-des-bouteilles-de-vin-magnum-jeroboam-mathusalem.

# BIBLIOGRAPHY

Cherry, Kendra. "Fluid vs. Crystallized Intelligence: Balancing Mental Flexibility and Accumulated Wisdom." Verywell Mind, July 11, 2024. https://www.verywellmind.com/fluid-intelligence-vs-crystallized-intelligence-2795004.

Christensen, Christian. "Did the Vikings Have a Written Language?" Scandinavia Facts. https://scandinaviafacts.com/did-the-vikings-have-a-written-language/.

———. "How Did the Vikings Bathe? You Might Be Surprised." Scandinavia Facts. https://scandinaviafacts.com/how-did-vikings-bathe/.

City of St. Augustine. "Our History." https://www.citystaug.com/693/Our-History.

Cohen, Stephen Michael. "Maria the Jewess." In *Shalvi/Hyman Encyclopedia of Jewish Women*. Jewish Women's Archive, June 25, 2021. https://jwa.org/encyclopedia/article/maria-jewess.

Colón, Priscilla. "Taíno Female Chiefs (Part 1)." YouTube video, October 28, 2022. https://www.youtube.com/watch?v=7vRVl3PO3u0.

Conan, Neal. "'No, We Straight': Obama Racially Bilingual." PBS *Talk of the Nation*, March 10, 2009. https://www.npr.org/transcripts/101661518.

Conga Chops. "A Brief History of the Bongos," February 5, 2021. https://www.congachops.com/blog-articles/2021/1/6/a-brief-history-of-the-bongos.

Cordon Bleu, Le. "What Are Pâtisserie, Boulangerie & Viennoiserie?" Le Cordon Bleu blog. https://www.cordonbleu.edu/news/what-are-patisserie-boulangerie-viennoiserie/en.

Cornwall Guide. https://www.cornwalls.co.uk/history/ancient.

Cowie, Del. "'Bling Bling': From Lil Wayne to Merriam-Webster." CBC Radio, May 9, 2017. https://www.cbc.ca/radio/q/bling-bling-from-lil-wayne-to-merriam-webster-1.4102195.

Crawfish Café. "The Differences between Crawfish, Crawdads, and Crayfish." January 10, 2022. https://www.crawfishcafe.com/the-differences-between-crawfish-crawdads-and-crayfish/.

Crowther, David. "Words Shakespeare Invented." *The History of England* (podcast), July 29, 2017. https://thehistoryofengland.co.uk/resource/words-shakespeare-invented/.

Crystal, David. "Old English," in "Discovering Literature: Medieval." British Library website. January 31, 2018. https://www.bl.uk/medieval-literature/articles/old-english.

Daily Meal. "Here's How Scrapple Might Have Gotten Its Name." March 24, 2023. https://www.thedailymeal.com/1131530/heres-how-scrapple-might-have-gotten-its-name/.

# BIBLIOGRAPHY

Day Translations. "Discovering the Arabic Influence in Spanish Language and Culture." Day Translations blog, February 12, 2018. https://www.daytranslations.com/blog/arabic-impact-spanish.

Dean, Sam. "The Etymology of Gumbo, Okra, and Oysters." *Bon Appétit* blog, February 8, 2013. https://www.bonappetit.com/test-kitchen/ingredients/article/the-etymology-of-gumbo-okra-and-oysters.

—. "The Etymology of the Word Rhubarb." *Bon Appétit* blog, March 21, 2013. https://www.bonappetit.com/test-kitchen/ingredients/article/the-etymology-of-the-word-rhubarb.

—. "On the Etymology of the Word Mayonnaise." *Bon Appétit* blog, April 4, 2013. https://www.bonappetit.com/test-kitchen/ingredients/article/on-the-etymology-of-the-word-mayonnaise#.

*Dictionary of the Scots Language*, s.v. "glamour." Scottish Language Dictionaries Ltd., 2004. https://www.dsl.ac.uk/entry/snd/glamour.

Dictionary.com, s.v. "buckaroo." https://www.dictionary.com/browse/buckaroo.

Digital Atlas of Ancient Life. "Greek & Latin in Botanical Terminology." Update of June 14, 2020. https://www.digitalatlasofancientlife.org/learn/embryophytes/botanical-terminology/.

DiMatteo, Chris. "Dutch Words in American English," 2016. cdmatteo.com. http://cdimatteo.com/english/dutch-words-in-american-english/.

Donoghue, Daniel G. "Beowulf in the Yard." *Harvard Magazine*, March 1, 2000. https://www.harvardmagazine.com/2000/03/beowulf-in-the-yard-html.

Doyle, Father Kenneth. "What Is the Origin of the Word 'Mass'?" The Boston-Pilot.com: *Echoes: A Forum of Catholic Thought,* July 5, 2018. https://www.thebostonpilot.com/opinion/article.asp?ID=182736.

Drasgow, Erik. "American Sign Language." In *Encyclopedia Britannica*, July 12, 2019. https://www.britannica.com/topic/American-Sign-Language.

Eigeland, Tor. *Al-Andalus* newsletter, print edition of *Saudi Aramco World*. AramcoWorld, 2005 archive. https://archive.aramcoworld.com/issue/200407/arabs.almonds.sugar.and.toledo-.compilation.htm.

Ellison, Ralph. "What America Would Be Without Blacks." *Time*, April 6, 1970. https://content.time.com/time/subscriber/article/0,33009,943970-1,00.html.

*Encyclopedia Britannica*. "Don Quixote, Novel by Cervantes." https://www.britannica.com/topic/Don-Quixote-novel.

—. "An Overview of the Settlement of Texas in the Early 19th Century," World History. https://www.britannica.com/video/167097/overview-settlement-Texas.

# BIBLIOGRAPHY

—. "St. Paul of Thebes, Christian Hermit." https://www.britannica.com/biography/Saint-Paul-of-Thebes.

English Heritage website. "Who Was St. Augustine?" *History and Stories.* https://www.english-heritage.org.uk/visit/places/st-augustines-abbey/history-and-stories/who-was-st-augustine/.

EnhanceMyVocabulary.com. "English Vocabulary Derived from Greek." https://www.enhancemyvocabulary.com.

Erichsen, Gerald. "Spain's Arab Connection Influenced the Language." ThoughtCo., July 3, 2019. https://www.thoughtco.com/spanishs-arab-connection-3078180.

Eupedia. "Interesting Facts About the Ancient Celts." https://www.eupedia.com/europe/celtic_trivia.shtml.

Explore Louisiana blogging team. "A Taste of a Louisiana Favorite: Beignets." https://www.explorelouisiana.com/blog/taste-louisiana-favorite-beignets.

EZGlot. "List of French Words of Latin Origin." https://www.ezglot.com/etymologies.php?l=fra&l2=lat.

Feinsilver, Lillian Mermin. "Yiddish Idioms in American English." *American Speech* 37, no. 3 (1962): 200–206. https://doi.org/10.2307/3090566.

Fox, Mira. "A Methuselah of Chardonnay? A Solomon of Champagne? How Big Wine Bottles Got So Biblical." *Forward*, April 12, 2024. https://forward.com/culture/602140/large-format-wine-bible-kings-israel/.

Freeman, Jan. "Did You Hear the One About 'Hysterical'?" *Throw Grammar from the Train* blog, February 9, 2012. http://throwgrammarfromthetrain.blogspot.com/2012/02/did-you-hear-one-about-hysterical.html.

Furlong, Amanda. "A New Major Exhibition at Mystic Seaport Museum, 'Entwined: Freedom, Sovereignty, and the Sea,'" Mystic Seaport Museum, March 20, 2024. https://mysticseaport.org/press-release/a-new-major-exhibition-at-mystic-seaport-museum-entwined-freedom-sovereignty-and-the-sea/.

Gallaudet University. "ASL and English Bilingualism." https://gallaudet.edu/asl-english-bilingualism/.

German Is Weird. "*Fremdscham.*" *Fun Facts and Trivia About the German Language* blog, October 3, 2021. https://germanisweird.com/fremdscham/.

Gillette, Sam. "Barack Obama Tried to Keep This a Secret from Michelle During Their Buckingham Palace Sleepover." *People*, updated June 5, 2018. https://www.yahoo.com/entertainment/barack-obama-tried-keep-secret-191109482.html.

# BIBLIOGRAPHY

Goldberg, Rabbi Efrem. "Learning to Say Genug Shoyn, Enough Already." RabbiEfremGoldberg.org. https://rabbiefremgoldberg.org/enough.

Gómez de Silva, Guido. *Elsevier's Concise Spanish Etymological Dictionary.* Amsterdam: Elsevier Science Publishers B.V., 1985. https://dokumen.pub/elseviers-concise-spanish-etymological-dictionary-hardcovernbsped-0444424407-9780444424402.html.

Green, Cynthia. "Wampum Was Massachusetts' First Legal Currency." *Jstor Daily,* November 23, 2017. https://daily.jstor.org/wampum-was-massachusetts-first-legal-currency/.

Greenspan, Jesse. "9 Things You May Not Know About Mardi Gras." History A&E Television Network, September 28, 2023. https://www.history.com/news/9-things-you-may-not-know-about-mardi-gras.

Gross, Terry. "Ranky Tanky Builds on the Music and Culture of Slave Descendants." National Public Radio: *Fresh Air,* December 12, 2017. https://www.npr.org/2017/12/12/569965570/ranky-tanky-leans-on-the-music-and-culture-of-slave-descendants.

Grundhauser, Eric. "What It Was Like to Seek Asylum in Medieval England." *Slate,* July 31, 2015. https://slate.com/human-interest/2015/07/in-medieval-england-fugitives-seeking-sanctuary-needed-only-to-get-themselves-to-church.html.

Grunstein, Erin. "Rice Krispie Treat Hamantaschen." Kosher.com. https://www.myjewishlearning.com/the-nosher/what-are-hamantaschen/.

Gullah Museum. "Rice Culture." https://www.gullahmuseumsc.com/new-page-2.

Gutman, Alejandro, and Beatriz Avanzati. The Language Gulper. https://languagesgulper.com/eng/Home.html.

—. "Latin." The Language Gulper. https://languagesgulper.com/eng/Latin.html.

Haines, Matt. "The Delicious History of a Cake Fit for a King." *Gambit* newsletter, January 3, 2022. https://www.nola.com/gambit/food_drink/the-delicious-history-of-a-cake-fit-for-a-king/article_c4bd0bb6-68e2-11ec-816d-6b3b5f8daba4.html.

Harrison, Mim. "So Long to the Skeuomorph? (Apple Takes a Bite.)" *Mim's the Word* (blog), November 1, 2012. http://mimharrison.blogspot.com/2012/11/so-long-to-skeuomorph-apple-takes-bite.html.

Hatic, Dana, and Hillary Dixler Canavan. "The King Cake Tradition, Explained." Eater, February 2, 2024. https://www.eater.com/22268353/king-cake-history-tradition-mardi-gras.

# BIBLIOGRAPHY

Haugen, Jason D. "Borrowed Borrowings: Nahuatl Loan Words in English." *Lexis—Journal in English Lexicology* 3 (July 27, 2009). https://doi.org/10.4000/lexis.638.

Hay, Mark. "The Hidden History of the Nutmeg Island That Was Traded for Manhattan." Atlas Obscura, February 28, 2019. https://www.atlasobscura.com/articles/island-traded-for-manhattan.

Hernandez Urraca, Vanessa. "The Hummingbird in Mexican Culture." Association of Avian Veterinarians, August 24, 2022. https://www.aav.org/news/615010/The-Hummingbird-in-Mexican-Culture.

Hilleary, Cecily. "Native Americans Gave Places, Animals, Plants Their Name." Voice of America Radio Network (VOA), November 17, 2017. https://www.voanews.com/a/native-american-tribes-gave-plates-animals-plants-their-names/4079554.html.

History. "Alhambra." August 21, 2018. https://www.history.com/topics/landmarks/alhambra.

Hoefnagel, Dick. "The Dartmouth Copy of John Eliot's Indian Bible (1639): Its Provenance." *Dartmouth College Library Bulletin.* https://www.dartmouth.edu/library/Library_Bulletin/Apr1993/LB-A93-Hoefnagel.html.

Hollandbeck, Andy. "Guy Fawkes Reunites Treason and Tradition." *In a Word, Language* blog. *The Saturday Evening Post,* November 9, 2018. https://www.saturdayeveningpost.com/2018/11/in-a-word-guy-fawkes-reunites-treason-and-tradition/.

*Holocaust Encyclopedia,* s.v. "pogroms." United States Holocaust Memorial Museum. https://encyclopedia.ushmm.org/content/en/article/pogroms#.

Hornberger, Matthew. "David Farragut: America's First Admiral." National Mall and Memorial Parks, National Park Service website. October 16, 2012. https://www.nps.gov/nama/blogs/david-farragut-america-s-first-admiral.htm.

Horwood, Catherine. "Glamour: Women, History, Feminism CAROL DYHOUSE." *Women's History Review* 21, no. 1 (2011): 166–67. https://doi.org/10.1080/09612025.2011.632926.

Hudson, Alison. "Religion in the Anglo-Saxon Kingdoms." British Library website. https://www.bl.uk/anglo-saxons/articles/religion-in-anglo-saxon-kingdoms.

Hunter, Dana. "The Origin of Amethysts May Leave You Tingly." *Scientific American* blog. February 28, 2019. https://blogs.scientificamerican.com/rosetta-stones/the-origin-of-amethysts-may-leave-you-tingly/.

# BIBLIOGRAPHY

- iDeal Wine. "Methuselahs, nebuchadnezzars . . . what's in a (bottle) name?" *Le Blog,* June 9, 2023. https://www.idealwine.info/methuselahs-nebuchadnezzars-whats-in-a-bottle-name/.
- Innes, Sim. "Celtic Languages." *Oxford Bibliographies,* August 6, 2019. https://www.oxfordbibliographies.com/view/document/obo-9780199772810/obo-9780199772810-0115.xml.
- *The Irish Post.* "Ten Words in the English Language That Come from Irish." June 1, 2015. https://www.irishpost.com/entertainment/ten-words-in-the-english-language-that-come-from-irish-53753.
- Jacobs, Jaap. "New Amsterdam & New York: What's in a Name?" New York Almanack, June 22, 2022. https://www.newyorkalmanack.com/2022/06/new-amsterdam-whats-in-a-name/.
- James, Edward. "Overview: The Vikings, 800 to 1066." BBC website. March 29, 2011. https://www.bbc.co.uk/history/ancient/vikings/overview_vikings_01.shtml.
- Jefferson, Thomas. Letter to J. Evelyn Denison, 9 November 1825. *Founders Online,* National Archives. https://founders.archives.gov/documents/Jefferson/98-01-02-5648.
- JewishHistory.org. "Yiddish." https://www.jewishhistory.org/yiddish-2/.
- Jones, Mary. "Jones' Celtic Encyclopedia," *Ancient Texts.* https://www.ancient-texts.org/library/celtic/jce/qceltic.html.
- Jordan, John-Erik. "139 Old Norse Words That Invaded The English Language." *Babbel* Magazine, October 9, 2019. https://www.babbel.com/en/magazine/139-norse-words.
- Kacian, Jim. *A Brief History of Haiku in the United States.* The Haiku Foundation. https://www.thehaikufoundation.org/omeka/files/original/8cd4850b0d-0799d6c3c72cd025fc8111.pdf.
- Kayal, Michelle. "Before Jambalaya, There Was Jollof Rice." Associated Press, April 23, 2013. As cited in HeraldNet. https://www.heraldnet.com/life/before-jambalaya-there-was-jollof-rice/.
- Kelly, John. *Everyday Etymology* (blog). Mashed Radish. https://mashedradish.com.
- —. *Etymology of the Day: Skosh* (blog). Mashed Radish, March 13, 2017. https://mashedradish.com/2017/03/13/etymology-of-the-day-skosh/.
- —. *Newsy Etymology: shogun, Tupperware, Secret Service, and interest rate* (blog). Mashed Radish, September 18, 2024. https://mashedradish.com/2024/09/18/shogun-tupperware-secret-service-interest-rate-word-origins/.

# BIBLIOGRAPHY

Khoury-Hanold, Layla. "What Is Praline?" Food Network Kitchen, November 15, 2022. https://www.foodnetwork.com/how-to/packages/food-network-essentials/what-is-praline.

Kibrick, Barry. "Schlemiel! Schlimazel! Hasenpfeffer Incorporated!" *The Huffington Post* blog, November 9, 2016. https://www.huffpost.com/entry/schlemiel-schlimazel-hase_b_8512450.

King, Ross. "Renaissance Discoveries: Latin." YouTube video, April 17, 2021. https://www.youtube.com/watch?v=ToABQcCRNxY&t=22s.

Kramer, Kyra Cornelius. "The Last Battle of the Prayer Book Rebellion." http://www.kyrackramer.com/2018/08/17/the-last-battle-of-the-prayer-book-rebellion/.

Kruse, John. "'All was delusion, nought was truth's—Faery Glamour." *British Fairies* blog, January 2, 2022. https://britishfairies.wordpress.com/2022/01/02/all-was-delusion-nought-was-truth-faery-glamour/comment-page-1/.

Kwan, Mildred. "All About Hominy." Familia Kitchen, August 2021. https://familiakitchen.com/all-about-hominy/.

Lagroue, Mary Claire. "What Is the Holy Trinity of Cajun Cooking?" Allrecipes, January 12, 2021. https://www.allrecipes.com/article/what-is-the-cajun-holy-trinity/.

Language Tsar. "How Similar Are Romanian and Spanish?" https://languagetsar.com/how-similar-are-romanian-and-spanish/.

Laskow, Sarah. "New Hampshire Mill Workers Invented a New Type of French." Atlas Obscura, February 8, 2016. https://www.atlasobscura.com/articles/new-hampshire-mill-workers-invented-a-new-type-of-french.

Leahy, Colleen. "'Ouisconsin': Why So Many Places in Wisconsin Have a French Name." Wisconsin Public Radio, December 14, 2021. https://www.wpr.org/culture/ouisconsin-why-so-many-places-wisconsin-have-french-name.

Lee, Madeleine. "Is English a Romance Language?" Rosetta Stone *Advice* post. https://blog.rosettastone.com/is-english-a-romance-language/.

Lehoux, Daryn. "Let Us Make the Effort: Science into Latin in Antiquity." *Isis: A Journal of the History of Science Society* 109, no. 2 (June 2018): 308–12. https://www.journals.uchicago.edu/toc/isis/2018/109/2.

LetThemTalkTV. "How the Vikings Changed the English Language." YouTube video, May 25, 2022. https://www.youtube.com/watch?v=9ZV1BOcGiV0.

Leveen, Steve. "Ross King's da Vinci Code: A New Reading on Leonardo, and How Leonardo Read." *Well-Read Life* blog, October 8, 2010. (Archived on typepad.com.)

# BIBLIOGRAPHY

Lévy, Carlos. "Cicero and the Creation of a Latin Philosophical Vocabulary." In *The Cambridge Companion to Cicero's Philosophy,* edited by Jed W. Atkins and Thomas Bénatouïl, 71–87. Cambridge: Cambridge University Press, 2021. https://doi.org/10.1017/9781108241649.007.

Lexico.com. "Five Events That Shaped the History of English: The Scandinavian Settlements." 2021. https://www.lexico.com/grammar/the-history-of-english.

Lewis Carroll Society of North America. "Lewis Carroll FAQ." LCSNA website. https://www.lewiscarroll.org/carroll/faq/.

Lewis, Miles Marshall. "With Wordplay, Wit and Ingenuity, Hip-Hop Artists Are Reshaping the Way We Speak." *The New York Times Magazine* (interactive), August 9, 2023. https://www.nytimes.com/interactive/2023/08/11/magazine/hip-hop-language-dope-cake-woke.html.

Literary Hub. "Isaac Bashevis Singer on the Particular Wonders of Writing in Yiddish," January 22, 2020. Excerpted from Ilan Stavans and Josh Lambert, eds., *How Yiddish Changed America and How America Changed Yiddish* (Brooklyn: Restless Books, 2020). https://lithub.com/isaac-bashevis-singer-on-the-particular-wonders-of-writing-in-yiddish/#:~:text=.

Library of Congress. "The American West, 1865–1900." U.S. History Primary Source Timeline. https://www.loc.gov/classroom-materials/united-states-history-primary-source-timeline/rise-of-industrial-america-1876-1900/american-west-1865-1900/.

—. "Buckaroos in Paradise: Ranching Culture in Northern Nevada, 1945 to 1982." https://www.loc.gov/collections/ranching-culture-in-northern-nevada-from-1945-to-1982/articles-and-essays/buckaroo-views-of-a-western-way-of-life/vaqueros/.

—. "The History of the Upper Midwest: An Overview." https://www.loc.gov/collections/pioneering-the-upper-midwest/articles-and-essays/history-of-the-upper-midwest-overview/.

—. "How Did the Squash Get Its Name?" *Everyday Mysteries* fact sheet, November 19, 2019. https://www.loc.gov/everyday-mysteries/agriculture/item/how-did-squash-get-its-name/#.

Luu, Chi. "Black English Matters." *JSTOR Daily,* February 12, 2020. https://daily.jstor.org/black-english-matters/.

Lyons, Dylan. "How Many People Speak English, and Where Is It Spoken?" *Babbel* Magazine, March 10, 2021. https://www.babbel.com/en/magazine/how-many-people-speak-english-and-where-is-it-spoken.

# BIBLIOGRAPHY

Marine Corps University. "Navajo Code Talkers in World War II." Reference Branch, USMC History Division, July 2006. https://www.usmcu.edu/Research/Marine-Corps-History-Division/People/Navajo-Code-Talkers-in-WWII/.

Marples, Megan. "Machu Picchu Has Been Called the Wrong Name for Over 100 Years. Historians Reveal Its True Name." CNN Travel, April 1, 2022. https://www.cnn.com/travel/article/machu-picchu-called-huayna-piccho-scn/index.html.

Marques, Nuno. "31 English Words That Are Actually French." *Babbel* Magazine, July 13, 2021. https://www.babbel.com/en/magazine/english-words-that-are-actually-french.

Marshall, Euan. "11 Fascinating Facts About the Portuguese Language." Culture Trip, July 14, 2017. https://theculturetrip.com/europe/portugal/articles/11-fascinating-facts-about-the-portuguese-language/.

Martinez, Erica. "How Scrapple Became a Pennsylvania Dutch Staple." Food Republic, June 6, 2023. https://www.foodrepublic.com/1285980/scrapple-history-pennsylvania-dutch-culture/.

Maston, Luke. Story of Mathematics. https://www.storyofmathematics.com.

Max Kade Institute for German-American Studies. "Pennsylvania Dutch Documentation Project." University of Wisconsin–Madison. https://mki.wisc.edu/research/language/pennsylvania-dutch-documentation-project/.

McCrum, Robert. "'Perfect Mind': On Shakespeare and the Brain." *Brain* 139, no. 12 (December 2016): 3310–13. https://doi.org/10.1093/brain/aww279.

———. "William Shakespeare: A Quintessentially American Author." *The Guardian*, April 9, 2016. https://www.theguardian.com/books/2016/apr/09/william-shakespeare-a-quintessentially-american-author.

McElroy, Daryn. "Press Play: Ranky Tanky Offer a Powerful Performance of 'Stand by Me' Using Traditional Gullah Techniques." Recording Academy, January 19, 2023. https://www.grammy.com/news/ranky-tanky-stand-by-me-performance-video-live-good-time-album-press-play.

McGlashen, Andy. "Are These Birds Better Than Computers at Predicting Hurricane Seasons?" *Audubon,* August 13, 2019. https://www.audubon.org/news/are-these-birds-better-computers-predicting-hurricane-seasons.

McGrath, Jane. "Did the Dutch Really Trade Manhattan for Nutmeg?" HowStuffWorks, April 20, 2009. https://history.howstuffworks.com/history-vs-myth/nutmeg-new-netherland.htm.

# BIBLIOGRAPHY

McWhorter, John. "Hearing the Music in Black American English." *The New York Times* Email Newsletter, November 9, 2023. https://www.nytimes.com/2023/11/09/opinion/black-english-purlie-victorious-broadway.html.

—. "How the Infiltration of French Words Changed English." *The Story of Human Language* lecture series. The Great Courses Daily, November 19, 2020. https://www.thegreatcoursesdaily.com/how-the-infiltration-of-french-words-changed-english/.

—. "San Francisco Schools Are Retiring 'Chief'." *The New York Times* Email Newsletter, June 7, 2022. https://www.nytimes.com/2022/06/07/opinion/san-francisco-chief.html.

—. "Why Did Latin Die Out?" *Lexicon Valley from Booksmart Studios* (podcast). September 12, 2022. https://lexiconvalley.substack.com/p/why-did-latin-die-out.

Meeks, Wayne A. "The Collision with Paganism." PBS Frontline: *From Jesus to Christ: The First Christians,* April 1998. https://www.pbs.org/wgbh/pages/frontline/shows/religion/first/paganism.html.

Merriam-Webster Wordplay. "15 Cheffy Words for Chefs (and Everyone Else)." *Merriam-Webster* online dictionary, July 31, 2024. https://www.merriam-webster.com/wordplay/culinary-words.

—. "A Passel of English Words from Yiddish." *Merriam-Webster* online dictionary. https://www.merriam-webster.com/wordplay/english-words-from-yiddish.

—. "10 Words from Pennsylvania German." Merriam-Webster online dictionary. https://www.merriam-webster.com/wordplay/10-words-from-pennsylvania-german.

Michelson, Bob. "Inshore Species Profile: Scup." *The Fisherman,* May 16, 2022. https://www.thefisherman.com/article/inshore-species-profile-scup/#.

Miller-Wilson, Kate. "29 English Words with Origins in Greek Mythology." YourDictionary. https://reference.yourdictionary.com/resources/roots-english-words-greek-mythology.html.

Mineo, Liz. "At Div School, Centuries-old Aztec Language Speaks to the Present." *The Harvard Gazette*, April 15, 2022. https://news.harvard.edu/gazette/story/2022/04/centuries-old-aztec-language-speaks-to-the-present/.

Morris, Bilal G. "Haints of Hoodoo: The Black Ghosts of the Gullah Geechee." NewsOne, October 25, 2022. https://newsone.com/4433221/haints-black-ghosts-of-the-gullah-geechee/.

# BIBLIOGRAPHY

Morris, Marc. "The Anglo-Saxons' Last Stand." History Extra, the website for *BBC History Magazine*, January 1, 2017. https://www.historyextra.com/period/norman/the-anglo-saxons-last-stand/.

Muhammad, Nylah Iqbal. "Chef Charly Pierre Pays Homage to Haitian Street Food in His New Orleans Restaurant." Andscape, January 19, 2023. https://andscape.com/features/chef-charly-pierre-fritai-new-orleans-restaurant/.

Murphy, Hugh. "Foods Indigenous to the Western Hemisphere: Squash." American Indian Health and Diet Project. https://aihd.ku.edu/foods/squash.html.

National Archives. "The Treaty of Guadalupe Hidalgo." Educator Resources, June 9, 2022. https://www.archives.gov/education/lessons/guadalupe-hidalgo#.

National Geographic Society. "Bayou." https://education.nationalgeographic.org/resource/bayou/.

—. "June 7, 1494 CE: Treaty of Tordesillas," October 4, 2022. https://education.nationalgeographic.org/resource/treaty-tordesillas/.

National Library of Medicine. "Greek Words in the Modern English Medical Vocabulary." National Institutes of Health. https://www.nlm.nih.gov/hmd/greek/greek_words.html.

National Museum of African American History and Culture. "Muslim Artifacts at the National Museum of African American History and Culture." https://nmaahc.si.edu/explore/stories/muslim-artifacts-national-museum-african-american-history-and-culture#.

National Park Service. "Log Cabins in America: The Finnish Experience (Teaching with Historic Places)." https://www.nps.gov/articles/000/log-cabins-in-america-the-finnish-experience-teaching-with-historic-places.htm#.

—. "The Mighty Peanut." Jimmy Carter National Historic Park, Georgia. October 17, 2023. https://www.nps.gov/jica/planyourvisit/the-mighty-peanut.htm.

—. "Sir Walter Ralegh." Fort Raleigh: National Historic Site, North Carolina. https://www.nps.gov/fora/learn/education/sir-walter-ralegh.htm#.

National Portrait Gallery. "Johnson's Literary Club." https://www.npg.org.uk/collections/search/group?grp=1201&page=1.

Naval History and Heritage Command. "Admiral." U.S. Navy website, May 13, 2014. https://www.history.navy.mil/research/library/online-reading-room/title-list-alphabetically/w/naval-traditions-names-of-rank/officer/admiral.

—. "Navajo Code Talkers' Dictionary, Revised 15 June 1945 (Declassified Under Department Of Defense Directive 5200.9)." U.S. Navy website, April 16, 2020. https://www.history.navy.mil/research/library/online-reading-room/title-list-alphabetically/n/navajo-code-talker-dictionary.html.

# BIBLIOGRAPHY

Neal, Joseph Clay. *Charcoal Sketches; Or, Scenes in a Metropolis.* Philadelphia: E.L. Carey and A. Hart, 1838. https://books.google.com/books?newbks=1&newbks_redir=0&id=Y8Tgvsg3vq4C&q=ouch#v=snippet&q=ouch&f=false.

Nelson, Ryan. "What Is the Vulgate? The Beginner's Guide." OverviewBible. September 7, 2018. https://overviewbible.com/vulgate/.

New Hampshire PBS. "Eastern Chipmunk—*Tamias striatus*." Wildlife Journal, Junior. https://nhpbs.org/wild/easternchipmunk.asp#.

*New World Encyclopedia.* "William Jones (philologist)." https://www.newworldencyclopedia.org/p/index.php?title=William_Jones.

New York Public Library. "Polonsky Exhibition of The New York Public Library's Treasures" permanent exhibition. Stephen A. Schwarzman Building, New York. https://www.nypl.org/spotlight/treasures.

Nordquist, Richard. "Doublets in English Language—Definition and Examples." ThoughtCo., August 20, 2018. https://www.thoughtco.com/what-are-doublets-words-1690477.

Northwest Indiana Latin Mass Community. "Latin Mass: History & FAQ's." https://nwilatin.org/history.

Nosowitz, Dan. "It's All Greek to You and Me, So What Is It to the Greeks?" Atlas Obscura, August 8, 2019. https://www.atlasobscura.com/articles/its-all-greek-to-me.

Oak Knoll Press. "Q & A with Reid Byers, author of *The Private Library*." *The Oak Knoll Biblio-Blog*, April 29, 2021. https://oakknollbooks.wordpress.com/2021/04/29/q-a-with-reid-byers-author-of-the-private-library/.

Ochoa, John. "Meet the First-Time GRAMMY Nominee: Ranky Tanky on the Lasting Influence of Gullah Music and Being Global Genre Ambassadors." Recording Academy, January 22, 2020. https://www.grammy.com/news/meet-first-time-grammy-nominee-ranky-tanky-lasting-influence-gullah-music-and-being.

O'Conner, Patricia T., and Stewart Kellerman. "Adjectives Galore." *Grammarphobia* blog, March 3, 2017. https://www.grammarphobia.com/blog/2017/03/galore.html.

—. "Cue Up or Queue Up a Video?" *Grammarphobia* blog, September 28, 2020. https://www.grammarphobia.com/blog/2020/09/cue-queue.html.

—. "Most of What You Think You Know About Grammar Is Wrong." *Smithsonian Magazine*, February 2013. https://www.smithsonianmag.com/arts-culture/most-of-what-you-think-you-know-about-grammar-is-wrong-4047445.

# BIBLIOGRAPHY

—. "A Quixotic Appeal." *Grammarphobia* blog. October 13, 2009. https://www.grammarphobia.com/blog/2009/10/a-quixotic-appeal.html.

—. "Sabotaging a Language Myth." *Grammarphobia* blog, September 24, 2010. https://www.grammarphobia.com/blog/2010/09/sabotage.html.

—. "Why Early Religions Are Pagan." *Grammarphobia* blog, February 4, 2019. https://www.grammarphobia.com/blog/2019/02/pagan.html.

*Online Nahuatl Dictionary*. Stephanie Wood, ed. Eugene, OR: University of Oregon, Wired Humanities Projects, College of Education. https://nahuatl.uoregon.edu/content/huitzilin.

Opala, Joseph A. "The Gullah: Rice, Slavery, and the Sierra-Leone-American Connection." Yale University: Gilder Lehrman Center for the Study of Slavery, Resistance, and Abolition. https://glc.yale.edu/sites/default/files/files/Gullah%20Language.pdf.

Oxford African American Studies Center. "The Banjo and African American Musical Culture." Oxford University Press. https://oxfordaasc.com/page/2351.

*Oxford English Dictionary*. "About the *Oxford Dictionary of African American English (ODAAE)*." Message from Henry Louis Gates, Jr., editor-in-chief, *ODAAE*. https://www.oed.com/discover/odaae?tl=true.

*Oxford English Dictionary*, s.v. "ouch," June 2024. https://doi.org/10.1093/OED/7739856398.

—, s.v. "praline," July 2023. https://doi.org/10.1093/OED/5623635622.

Oxford Languages. "The Linguistic and Cultural Influence of Hip-Hop and Rap: Findings of the Oxford Dictionary of African American English Project." YouTube video, October 29, 2024. https://www.youtube.com/watch?v=fpkDALJEW0Y.

Oxford Reference, s.v. "marzipan." Online public content from Cresswell, Julia, *Oxford Dictionary of Word Origins*. 3rd ed. Oxford University Press, 2021. https://www.oxfordreference.com/display/10.1093/acref/9780198868750.001.0001/acref-9780198868750-e-3117.

Oxford Royale. "Why Is English So Hard to Learn?" https://www.oxford-royale.com/articles/learning-english-hard/.

Pak, Amy. "The History of Marzipan." Home School in the Woods Publishing blog, December 5, 2020. https://store.homeschoolinthewoods.com/blogs/words-from-the-woods/the-history-of-marzipan.

Parks, Shoshi. "What the Color 'Haint Blue' Means to the Descendants of Enslaved Africans." Atlas Obscura, January 14, 2020. https://www.atlasobscura.com/articles/what-haint-blue-means-to-descendants-enslaved-africans.

# BIBLIOGRAPHY

Pavone, Pietro. "*Jacaranda mimosifolia.*" Translated by Mario Beltramini. *Monaco Nature Encyclopedia.* https://www.monaconatureencyclopedia.com/jacaranda-mimosifolia/?lang=en.

PBS. "Horses in North America: A Comeback Story." *Nature* (blog), February 25, 2022. https://www.pbs.org/wnet/nature/blog/american-horses-horses-in-north-america-a-comeback-story/#.

—. "Interview with the Filmmakers": interview with Ken Burns on the 2001 documentary miniseries *Jazz.* https://www.pbs.org/kenburns/jazz/q-a-with-filmmakers.

—. "Murder at Harvard: Boston Brahmins." *American Experience.* https://www.pbs.org/wgbh/americanexperience/features/murder-boston-brahmins/.

Pelo, June. "The Log Cabin Tradition." Swedish Finn Historical Society, 2020. https://www.swedishfinnhistoricalsociety.org/the-log-cabin-tradition/.

*Pennsylvania Dutch Dictionary.* s.v. "*der Pannhaas.*" https://www.padutchdictionary.com/entries/nouns/Pannhaas.html.

Peterson, Herman A. "Review of *Literacy and Intellectual Life in the Cherokee Nation, 1820–1906*, by James W. Parins." *Tribal College Journal of American Indian Higher Education* 27, no. 1 (Fall 2015). https://tribalcollegejournal.org/literacy-and-intellectual-life-in-the-cherokee-nation-1820-1906/.

Poirier, Regine. "Word of the Week: Kummerspeck." GermanyinUSA, October 19, 2021. https://germanyinusa.com/2021/10/19/word-of-the-week-kummerspeck/.

Poole, Robert M. "What Became of the Taíno?" *Smithsonian* Magazine, October 2011. https://www.smithsonianmag.com/travel/what-became-of-the-taino-73824867/.

Poort, Eva D., and Jennifer M. Rodd. "A Database of Dutch-English Cognates, Interlingual Homographs and Translation Equivalents." *PsyArXiv Preprints,* December 18, 2018, edited June 28, 2021. doi: 10.31234/osf.io/hjn8b.

Price, Todd A. "Rooted in History: The Haitian Influence on New Orleans Cuisine." USA TODAY Network, as featured in *Daily Advertiser.* December 4, 2019. https://www.theadvertiser.com/story/life/2019/12/04/new-orleans-food-haitian-influence/.

Princeton University Library's Cataloging Documentation. "Cataloging Biblical Materials: Summary Descriptions of Versions of the Bible." Princeton University Library. https://library.princeton.edu/departments/tsd/katmandu/bible/versions.html.

# BIBLIOGRAPHY

Quinion, Michael. "Balderdash and flummery." World Wide Words, November 23, 1996. https://www.worldwidewords.org/articles/welsh.htm.

—. "Gallimaufry." World Wide Words, December 3, 2011. https://www.worldwidewords.org/weirdwords/ww-gal1.htm.

Rambaran-Olm, Mary, and Erik Wade. "The Many Myths of the Term 'Anglo-Saxon.'" *Smithsonian* Magazine, July 14, 2021. https://www.smithsonianmag.com/history/many-myths-term-anglo-saxon-180978169/.

Real Food Encyclopedia. "Kumquats." FoodPrint. https://foodprint.org/real-food/kumquats/.

Rocket Gardens. "Swede vs Turnip? Diary of a Rocket Gardener." https://www.rocketgardens.co.uk/swede-vs-turnip-diary-of-a-rocket-gardener/.

Rose, Sarah. "The Great British Tea Heist." *Smithsonian* Magazine, March 9, 2010. https://www.smithsonianmag.com/history/the-great-british-tea-heist-9866709/.

Rothwell, William. "Anglo-French and the Anglo-Norman Dictionary." Preface to the 2006 print edition of the *Anglo-Norman Dictionary A-E*. 2nd ed. UK: Modern Humanities Research Association. Reprinted online in 2017. https://anglo-norman.net/anglo-french/.

Sahgal, Neha, Jonathan Evans, Ariana Monique Salazar, Kelsey Jo Starr, and Manolo Corichi. "Attitudes About Caste." *Religion in India: Tolerance and Segregation*. Pew Research Center: June 29, 2021. https://www.pewresearch.org/religion/2021/06/29/attitudes-about-caste/.

Sala, Marius, Rebecca Posner, et al. "Romance Languages." In *Encyclopedia Britannica*, November 2, 2022. https://www.britannica.com/topic/Romance-languages.

Salazar, Danica. "From Anime to Zen: Japanese Words in the OED." *Oxford English Dictionary*. https://www.oed.com/discover/japanese-words-in-the-oed/.

Saxey, Roderick II. "The Greek Language Through Time." Department of Linguistics, Linguistics 450, Brigham Young University, updated September 6, 1999. https://linguistics.byu.edu/classes/Ling450ch/reports/greek.html.

Schepens, Job Johannes, Ton Dijkstra, Franc Grootjen, and Walter J.B. van Heuven. "Cross-Language Distributions of High Frequency and Phonetically Similar Cognates." *PLOS ONE* (May 10, 2013). https://doi.org/10.1371/journal.pone.0063006.

Schleip, Sara. "Small Latin and Less Greek: A Look at the Inkhorn Controversy." *Shakespeare & Beyond*, blog of the Folger Shakespeare Library.

# BIBLIOGRAPHY

April 5, 2019. https://shakespeareandbeyond.folger.edu/2019/04/05/inkhorn-controversy-latin-greek-english-words/.

Sellars, Luana M. Graves. "Are You a Gullah or Geechee?" *Lowcountry Gullah* blog, July 31, 2019. https://lowcountrygullah.com/are-you-gullah-geechee-whats-the-difference/.

Sententiae Antiquae. "Greek Nostos and English Nostalgia." *Sententiae Antiquae* blog, August 12, 2018. https://sententiaeantiquae.com/2018/08/12/greek-nostos-and-english-nostalgia/.

Shakespeare Birthplace Trust. "Shakespeare's Words." https://www.shakespeare.org.uk/explore-shakespeare/shakespedia/shakespeares-words/.

Shako:wi Cultural Center. "Wampum: Validating the Spoken Message." Oneida Indian Nation. https://www.oneidaindiannation.com/shakowiculturalcenter/#.

Siciliano-Rosen, Laura. "Jambalaya." In *Encyclopedia Britannica*, July 5, 2024. https://www.britannica.com/topic/jambalaya.

Simon & Simon. "Legal English—The Use of Legal Doublets." Blog of Simon & Simon business language training courses, January 22, 2019. https://www.simonandsimon.co.uk/blog/legal-english-the-use-of-legal-doublets.

SKY History. "Old Norse Words We Use Every Day." A&E Networks. https://www.history.co.uk/shows/vikings/articles/old-norse-words-we-use-every-day.

Small, Andrew. "Why Is Britain Called Britain?" *These Islands,* December 23, 2017. https://www.these-islands.co.uk/publications/i281/why_is_britain_called_britain.aspx.

Smith, Chrysti M. "Wild West Words: Banjo, Eskimo/Husky, and Vigilante." *Distinctly Montana,* December 20, 2017. https://www.distinctlymontana.com/wild-west-words-banjo-eskimohusky-and-vigilante.

Southern Cast Iron. "As New Orleans as Étouffée." May 31, 2022. https://southerncastiron.com/new-orleans-etouffee-devin-smith/.

Spiropoulou, Angeliki. "'On Not Knowing Greek': Virginia Woolf's Spatial Critique of Authority," *Interdisciplinary Literary Studies* 4, no. 1 (Fall 2002): 1–19. https://www.jstor.org/stable/41208803?read-now=1&seq=8#page_scan_tab_contents.

St. Pierre. "What Is Brioche?—10 Things You Need to Know About Brioche." St. Pierre bakery company blog. https://stpierrebakery.co.uk/blog/10-things-to-know-about-brioche/.

Stahls, Paul F., Jr. "Jambalaya." *Louisiana Life* Magazine, January 1, 2009. https://www.louisianalife.com/jambalaya/.

# BIBLIOGRAPHY

Stanton, Mike. "Ocean State's Most Abundant Fish Slowly Finds Local Tables." *ecoRI News,* November 5, 2022. https://ecori.org/ocean-states-most-abundant-fish-slowly-finds-local-tables/.

Stravinskas, Rev. Peter M.J. "Roses, The Rose, and the Rosary." *The Catholic World Report,* October 1, 2021. https://www.catholicworldreport.com/2021/10/01/roses-the-rose-and-the-rosary/.

Stroud, Kevin. "Beowulf and Other Viking Ancestors." *The History of English* podcast. Episode 42, May 6, 2014. https://historyofenglishpodcast.com/2014/05/06/episode-42-beowulf-and-other-viking-ancestors/.

—. "Bloody Axes and a Battle Royal." *The History of English* podcast. Episode 52, November 7, 2014. https://historyofenglishpodcast.com/2014/11/07/episode-52-bloody-axes-and-a-battle-royal/.

—. "Greek, Phoenicia and the Alphabet." *The History of English* podcast. Episode 13, October 17, 2012. https://historyofenglishpodcast.com/2012/10/17/episode-13-greece-phoenicia-and-the-alphabet-2/.

—. "The Greek Word Horde." *The History of English* podcast. Episode 14, November 1, 2012. https://historyofenglishpodcast.com/2012/11/01/episode-14-the-greek-word-horde/.

—. "A Rude and Rusty Language." *The History of English* podcast. Episode 147, April 28, 2021. https://historyofenglishpodcast.com/2021/04/28/episode-147-a-rude-and-rusty-language/.

—. "The Second French Invasion." *The History of English* podcast. Episode 99, September 9, 2017. https://historyofenglishpodcast.com/2017/09/09/episode-99-the-second-french-invasion/.

—. "Vikings Among the English and French." *The History of English* podcast. Episode 49, September 17, 2014. https://historyofenglishpodcast.com/2014/09/17/episode-49-vikings-among-the-english-and-french/.

Syme, Holger. "People Being Stupid About Shakespeare III." *Dispositio* blog, July 18, 2011. http://www.dispositio.net/archives/368.

Szmigiera, M. "The Most Spoken Languages Worldwide in 2021." *Statista,* March 30, 2021. https://www.statista.com/statistics/266808/the-most-spoken-languages-worldwide/.

Tasca, Cecilia, Mariangela Rapetti, Mauro Giovanni Carta, and Bianca Fadda. "Women and Hysteria in the History of Mental Health." *Clinical Practice and Epidemiology in Mental Health* 8 (2012): 110-19. https://pubmed.ncbi.nlm.nih.gov/23115576/.

# BIBLIOGRAPHY

Texas Parks & Wildlife. "Common Raccoon (*Procyon lotor*)." Wildlife Fact Sheets. https://tpwd.texas.gov/huntwild/wild/species/raccoon/.

Thavis, John. "Vatican Prepares Three Alternative Endings for Dismissal at Mass." *National Catholic Reporter,* October 20, 2008. https://www.ncronline.org/news/vatican-prepares-three-alternative-endings-dismissal-mass.

Thesaurus.com. "Do English Nouns Have a Gender?" May 16, 2012. https://www.thesaurus.com/e/grammar/oldenglishgender/.

Thomas, Bethan, and Jaymelouise Hudspith. "10 Common English Words You May Not Know Came from Welsh." *North Wales News,* January 2, 2020. https://www.dailypost.co.uk/news/north-wales-news/10-common-english-words-you.

ThoughtCo. Team. "How Is W Pronounced in French?" ThoughtCo., July 1, 2019. https://www.thoughtco.com/french-pronunciation-of-w.

—. "Terms of Enrichment: How French Has Influenced English." ThoughtCo., November 4, 2019. https://www.thoughtco.com/how-french-has-influenced-english.

Tibbetts, John H. "Living Soul of Gullah." *Coastal Heritage* 14, no. 4 (Spring 2000): 3–12. https://www.scseagrant.org/wp-content/uploads/Coastal-Heritage-Spring-2000.pdf.

Tolkien Society. "Anglo-Saxon, Part One." *The Tolkien Society Education Packs*. https://www.tolkiensociety.org/app/uploads/2016/11/Anglo-Saxon-Part-1.pdf.

Transparent Language. "Cognates." *Norwegian Language Blog,* posted by kari. May 22, 2009. https://blogs.transparent.com/norwegian/author/kari/.

Tufano, Victoria M. "When Did We Start Celebrating Mass in Latin?" *U.S. Catholic,* June 18, 2010. https://uscatholic.org/articles/201006/when-did-we-start-celebrating-mass-in-latin/.

TV Trope. "Characters / Don Quixote." https://tvtropes.org/pmwiki/pmwiki.php/Characters/DonQuixote.

Ulm, J. Wes. "Table of Germanic Vocabulary Cognates Across English, German, Dutch, Norwegian, Swedish, and Danish." 2016. https://wesulm.angelfire.com/languages/common_germanic_vocabtable.htm.

UNESCO. "Did You Know?: The Evolution of the Arabic Language in the Silk Roads." Silk Roads Programme. https://en.unesco.org/silkroad/content/did-you-know-evolution-arabic-language-silk-roads.

University of Maine. "Teaching Canada. Culture Focus: Acadia, Acadians." https://umaine.edu/teachingcanada/culture-focus-acadia-acadians/.

# BIBLIOGRAPHY

USA TODAY. "Barack and Michelle Obama Dined Here." January 9, 2017. https://www.usatoday.com/picture-gallery/travel/experience/food-and-wine/2017/01/09/barack-and-michelle-obama-dined-here/.

Vachon, Pamela. "Marzipan in My Veins: A History of the Almond Candy." Salon newsletter, January 9, 2021. https://www.salon.com/2021/01/09/marzipan-in-my-veins-a-history-of-the-almond-candy_partner/.

Valenti, Denise. "Lozano Discusses 'An American Language: The History of Spanish in the United States.'" Princeton University: News, November 6, 2018. https://www.princeton.edu/news/2018/11/06/lozano-discusses-american-language-history-spanish-united-states.

Vatican News. "The Chanting of the Gospel in Greek in Certain Papal Celebrations." Office for the Liturgical Celebrations of the Supreme Pontiff. https://www.vatican.va/news_services/liturgy/details/ns_lit_doc_20091117_canto-vangelo_en.html.

Vaughn, Grace Lenehan. "The History of the Jukebox: From the 1880s to Today." Wide Open Country, May 6, 2021. https://www.wideopencountry.com/history-of-the-jukebox/.

Vermette, David. "The Other Side of The Cotton: Franco-Americans in the Textile Industry." French North America blog, August 5, 2015. https://french-northamerica.blogspot.com/2015/08/the-other-side-of-cotton-franco.html.

Vespe, Jim. "It Was John Glenn Who Popularized the Word '"Glitch'." *Smithsonian Air & Space* Magazine, October 2019. https://www.smithsonianmag.com/air-space-magazine/just-right-word-180973113/.

Videen, Hana. *Old English Wordhord* blog. https://oldenglishwordhord.com.

The Viking Herald. "Viking King Harald Bluetooth Was a Major Inspiration for Technology Developers. Here's the Story." 2022. https://thevikingherald.com/article/viking-king-harald-bluetooth-was-a-major-inspiration-for-technology-developers-here-s-the-story/5.

Ville de Québec. "Heritage: Champlain, Founder of Quebec." https://www.ville.quebec.qc.ca/en/citoyens/patrimoine/quartiers/vieux_quebec/interet/champlain.aspx.

Visit Greece. "Greek Language." https://www.pointgreece.com/greek-language/.

Waugh, Alexander. "That 'Famous Persecutor of Priscian': Oxford, Shakespeare and the Repurification of English." De Vere Society newsletter, April 2020. https://deveresociety.co.uk/wp-content/uploads/2015/12/NL_2020_27_2_April_FINAL_05Apr2020AW.pdf.

# BIBLIOGRAPHY

Weisberger, Mindy. "How Did the Milky Way Get Its Name?" LiveScience. November 7, 2016. https://www.livescience.com/56756-milky-way-name-origin.html.

Westport Library. "Opossums: Natural Science." *Westport Library Resource Guides*. https://westportlibrary.libguides.com/opossums.

Weyde, Ber. "Manx Gaelic Phrasebook–26,000 Examples." As Manx as the Hills website. http://asmanxasthehills.com/manx-gaelic-phrasebook-26000-examples/.

What's Cooking America. "Beignet History and Recipe." https://whatscookingamerica.net/history/beignetshistory.htm.

White, René Locklear. "Scuppernong Muscadine Grape—Talking Paper." Presentation by a Lumbee Tribe member to the Smithsonian National Museum of the American Indian. September 8–9, 2017. https://sanctuaryonthetrail.org/uploads/3/4/7/3/34730008/muscadine_grape.pdf.

Whitehurst, Katie. "Revolution and Republic, 1836–1845." Texas PBS: *Explore Texas by Historical Eras*. https://texasourtexas.texaspbs.org/the-eras-of-texas/revolution-and-republic/.

Whitman, Mark. "Climbing Huayna Picchu—Get The Best View of Machu Picchu." Machu Picchu Trek Guide. https://www.machupicchutrek.net/huayna-picchu/.

Wikipedia. "Indo-European Vocabulary." https://en.wikipedia.org/wiki/Indo-European_vocabulary.

Winford, Donald. "The Origins of African American Vernacular English: Beginnings." In Jennifer Bloomquist, Lisa J. Green, and Sonja L. Lanehart, eds., *The Oxford Handbook of African American Languag*e (Oxford Academic online edition: August 6, 2015), 85–104. https://doi.org/10.1093/oxfordhb/9780199795390.013.5.

Woloson, Wendy. "Pennsylvania German Broadsides: Windows into an American Culture." Library Company of Philadelphia exhibition, 2006. https://www.librarycompany.org/broadsides/section1b.htm.

Woodman, Stephen. "Mexico's Hidden Arabic Heritage." Culture Trip. August 22, 2017. https://theculturetrip.com/north-america/mexico/articles/mexicos-hidden-arabic-heritage/.

Worldmapper. "Spread of the Greek Language." Map No. 568, accessed October 26, 2022. https://worldmapper.org/maps/spread-of-the-greek-language/.

Yivo Institute for Jewish Research. "Learning Yiddish." https://yivo.org/Yiddish#:~:text.

# BIBLIOGRAPHY

YourDictionary. "Biography: Canute I the Great." https://biography.yourdictionary.com/canute-i-the-great.

Zimmer, Ben. "How 'Mojo' Got Its Magic Working." *The Wall Street Journal*, October 4, 2018. https://www.wsj.com/articles/how-mojo-got-its-magic-working-1538665006.

——. "'Levee': A Raised River Bank–or a King's Awakening." *The Wall Street Journal*, September 2, 2021. https://www.wsj.com/articles/levee-a-raised-river-bankor-a-kings-awakening-11630619688.

Ziogas, Ioannis. "Famous Last Words: Caesar's Prophecy on the Ides of March." *Antichthon* 50 (2016): 134–53. doi:10.1017/ann.2016.9 =.

Zuras, Matthew. "A History of Ketchup, America's Favorite Condiment." Epicurious. June 30, 2023. https://www.epicurious.com/ingredients/history-of-ketchup.

# ACKNOWLEDGMENTS

A casual question in an email conversation several years ago kickstarted this book. Ross King, an author I admire immensely, wanted to know how my writing was coming along. That was all the encouragement I needed.

George Gibson gave me the confidence to see that this just might be the smart word book he said it was. Having this highly regarded publishing executive believe in me is but one of many generous gestures he has graced me with over the years.

My editor, Tina St. Pierre, she of the eagle eye and astute mind, caught me out every time I needed to be. I am so fortunate to be the recipient of her talent and dedication.

I am also grateful to Thea Michele Smith, who fact-checked the chapter on Gullah with an astuteness that can only be called breathtaking. Many thanks to Ralph Eubanks for connecting us.

Another terrific connector was Sally Barrett, an administrator at my beloved alma mater, Allegheny College, who put me in touch with an equally beloved English professor from many years ago. Paul Zolbrod gave me the guidance I needed to present the story of the Navajo Code Talkers. His own love of language had led him to a professorship at Diné College in New Mexico, where he spent decades immersed in the Navajo language and culture—and knew some of the Code Talkers.

My thanks to UCLA professor Adam Bradley, an advisory board member of the *Oxford Dictionary of African American English* project

## ACKNOWLEDGMENTS

team, for reviewing my writeup of hip-hop. Alli Torban, a data visualist, introduced me to "choropleth," which I introduced to you in the Greek section.

Tom Morris, the most ebullient public philosopher on the planet, checked me on my ancient Greeks and Romans (he speaks both their languages). To Dr. Kieran O'Mahony, *go raibh maith agat*—an Irish thank-you—for his prodigious knowledge of Celtic cultures.

Priscilla Colón and Lorie Roule, two extraordinary advocates of languages, were invaluable reviewers. They offered not only their professional insights but also their friendship, giving me support and kindness beyond measure. As Priscilla would say in her heritage Taíno, *jajóm*—thank you.

I add these friends to the many others who are always ready to serve up inspiration and emotional sustenance: Alicia Biskup, Patrice Brierty, Leigh Brown, Vikki Corliss, Karen Granger, Suzanne Hogan, Kim Holt, Mercedes Lawry, Carolyn Martine, Sarah McBrearty, Susan Place, and La Trease Shaw. Andrea Syverson cheered me on (and up) as only she could. And Dee Moustakas was a steadfast sounding board whose all-in support made all the difference in so many ways.

Tabitha Lahr designed this book and did the beautiful, meticulous job I knew she would. Many thanks to her as well to Joel and Laura Pitney, Sayde Walker, and the entire team at Launch My Book, for doing just that.

I am indebted (deeply!) to Steve Leveen, the founder of the America the Bilingual project, for so many opportunities over the years that it would take a spreadsheet to capture them all. When Steve invited me to join his project, my fascination with English was reignited as I dipped my toe into Spanish (I'm now up to about my calf). I am so honored to be published by America the Bilingual Press.

A favorite word in Spanish I learned early on is *siempre*—always. I thank those who will be the center of my world *siempre*: Marcella and Joe Aud; Gisela and Federico Formica, and their beautiful daughters; my sister Denise, who epitomizes *fidelis*; and my husband, Nigel, who in his quiet British way, has always believed I could.

# INDEX OF WORDS

## A
admiral, 51
aficionado, 144
alcohol, 53
alfalfa, 50
algebra, 54
alkali, 50
alphabet, 59
amethyst, 66
amuse-bouche, 77
angel, 32
anime, 182
antipathy, 63
antiquity, 72
apathy, 63
arcane, 27
arithmetic, 62
ark, 27
armada, 88
armadillo, 143
armoire, 149
armor, 149
arriviste, 71
arsenal, 54
asperity, 91
auspicious, 107
avatar, 116
average, 54
avocado, 129

## B
badlands, 183
bagel, 109
bail, 73
bailiff, 73
bain-marie, 185
banana, 158
banjo, 159
banshee, 19
baptism, 32
barbarian, 60
barbecue, 128
bask, 40
bayou, 165
beignet, 168
berserk, 44
bildungsroman, 172
bill, 33
bling, 161
bonanza, 143
bongo, 158
book-wrapt, 106
boondocks, 183
Brahman, 117
bread, 25
brioche, 168
brogue, 19
buckaroo, 142
bull, 33
bump, 105
bupkes, 102
butte, 163

## C
cache, 163
cachet, 25

## INDEX OF WORDS

cafeteria, 143
cake, 43
cakewalk, 156
calamity, 72
candy, 51
canoe, 128
canyon, 143
cardigan, 18
Caribbean, 114
carte blanche, 77
caters, 105
catharsis, 63
cay, 128
c'est la vie, 77
chaos, 59
chaparral, 143
chaps, 142
chili pepper, 129
chill, 156
chipmunk, 127
chocolate, 129
choropleth, 63
choux, 168
chutzpah, 177
cocoa, 129
coffee, 55
colonizing, 111
come, 25
conclave, 34
condor, 129
conjugal, 11
consecrate, 32
cookie, 118
coracle, 18
cordial, 11
corgi, 18
corral, 143

cosmos, 59
cosplay, 182
courage, 11
courtesy, 3
cow, 105
coyote, 129
creole, 152
crevasse, 163
croissant, 168
crooked, 41
cruller, 118
cuisine, 75
curate, 190

### D

daisy, 28
dank, 41
de rigueur, 88
decadent, 167
déclassé, 71
déjà vu, 71
democracy, 59
deracinate, 109
desperado, 88
deus ex machina, 63
die, 43
dissing, 155
dog, 9
doppelgänger, 172
dreck, 176
dreg, 41
dunk, 171
dystopia, 65

### E

echolalia, 61
egg, 43

élan, 71
elbow, 109
embargo, 88
embrace, 109
emoji, 182
empathy, 192
engine, 11
enmesh, 105
enthrall, 43
equine, 9
etiquette, 74
étouffée, 168
etymology, 62
eucharist, 66
evangelical, 32
explore, 88
extreme, 90
extremity, 72

### F

fable, 190
faithful, 32
fasnacht, 170
ferhoodle, 171
flummery, 20
foliage, 91
foot, 25
force majeure, 77
foreign, 1
fortnight, 28
freckle, 44
fricassee, 167
furious, 61
futz, 176

### G

galaxy, 61

## INDEX OF WORDS

gallant, 75
gallimaufry, 75
galore, 18
garble, 55
gargle, 74
gargoyle, 74
gasp, 44
gazelle, 49
gelato, 9
gemütlichkeit, 172
generous, 108
genteel, 74
geometry, 62
gerbil, 49
gestalt, 172
get, 41
ghosted, 162
gift, 44
giraffe, 49
give, 41
glamour, 18
glitch, 170
go, 25
go-between, 105
goober, 155
gospel, 32
granite, 11
green-eyed monsters, 105
grill, 156
grime, 41
guacamole, 129
guano, 184

**H**
haiku, 181
haint blue, 158
halogen, 11
hamartia, 63
hammock, 128
hand, 25
hant, 158
Hellenic, 58
hermit, 66
hilarious, 64
hippocampus, 64
hominy, 138
honcho, 181
hosanna, 32
hubris, 63
humor (v.), 108
hurricane, 128
hyperbola, 62
hyperbole, 62
hysterical, 63

**I, J**
imprimatur, 33
infidel, 32
ingenious, 11
inkhorn, 91
jacaranda, 183
jail, 73
jambalaya, 168
jaunty, 74
je ne sais quoi, 76
jerky, 129
jeroboam, 185
joie de vivre, 77
joust, 11
juggernaut, 117
juke, 159

**K**
kaput, 173
keen, 19
ken, 28
kerfuffle, 18
ketchup, 184
kilt, 45
kindergarten, 147
kitchen, 156
klutz, 176
knee, 9
kumbaya, 152
Kummerspeck, 174
kumquat, 184
kvell, 176
kvetch, 176

**L**
lagniappe, 129
lasso, 142
leitmotif, 172
levee, 169
llama, 130
looseleft, 106
loot, 116
lothario, 144

**M**
Madeira, 11
magazine, 55
maize, 128
marchpane, 186
marzipan, 186
mattress, 48
maven, 177
mayonnaise, 75
mellifluous, 9

## INDEX OF WORDS

mesa, 143
miniature, 98
mission, 35
mocha, 55
mogul, 112
mojito, 145
mojo, 158
mollify, 99
monsoon, 55
monumental, 109
Moors, 49
moose, 127
mot juste, 71
muck, 41
muskrat, 127
mustang, 142

**N, O**
nabob, 117
nausea, 66
nebbish, 176
noblesse oblige, 77
nom de guerre, 77
nom de plume, 77
noodge, 176
nose, 9
nosh, 176
nostalgia, 66
ocelot, 129
old, 10
ouch, 171
outlaw, 44
over, 10

**P**
pagan, 32
pajama, 117

palimpsest, 181
pander, 109
panicked, 61
parable, 62
parablepsis, 99
parabola, 62
pareidolia, 99
pasty, 20
pathos, 63
peasant, 73
pemmican, 138
penguin, 18
pentagon, 62
phobia, 61
phronesis, 63
picaresque, 144
pinochle, 173
plotz, 176
poet, 97
poetaster, 97
pogrom, 175
poltergeist, 172
pomegranate, 11
pope, 33
poplin, 33
poppycock, 119
possum, 127
potato, 128
prairie, 163
praline, 167
Presbyterian, 10
propaedeutic, 63
propaganda, 34
psalm, 32
puma, 130
pundit, 116

**Q, R**
queue, 74
quinine, 129
quinoa, 129
quixotic, 145
raccoon, 127
ransack, 44
ranting, 105
red-letter day, 97
remorseless, 108
Renaissance, 87
restaurant, 76
rhapsodic, 80
rhubarb, 60
ring shout, 160
rodeo, 142
rosary, 35
rotisserie, 167
rotunda, 91
rubrication, 98
rutabaga, 115

**S**
sabotage, 73
sacred, 32
sacrosanct, 36
saffron, 48
salad days, 105
salami, 11
salvation, 32
sanctuary, 36
savagery, 108
savannah, 128
scab, 41
scant, 42
scare, 42
schadenfreude, 172

## INDEX OF WORDS

scherenschnitte, 171
schlemiel, 177
schlemizal, 177
schlep, 177
schmaltz, 177
schmear, 176
schmooze, 176
schnoz, 177
schtick, 177
scorch, 42
scot, 45
scrapple, 170
scrub, 42
scuffle, 105
scup, 138
scuppernong grape, 138
seersucker, 117
senate, 10
senescence, 10
senile, 10
senior, 10
seven, 9
sherbert, 51
sherbet, 51
shogun, 181
shout-out, 160
shtikl, 175
side hustle, 156
sierra, 143
siesta, 146
skate, 43
skeuomorph, 99
skill, 42
skillet, 42
skosh, 183
skunk, 127

sky, 42
slaughter, 44
sleuth, 44
slew, 18
smitten, 90
smuggle, 88
snollygoster, 171
snoop, 118
sofa, 3
spritz, 171
squash, 138
stampede, 142
stoops, 115
strange bedfellows, 105
sugar, 51
surrender, 25
swede, 115
sympathy, 63
synecdoche, 63
syrup, 51

## T

take, 44
tango, 158
tantalized, 61
taps, 142
tariff, 56
ten-gallon hat, 143
thou, 9
ticket, 74
tomato, 129
tradition, 74
treason, 74
trifle, 20
triskaidekaphobia, 63

truncate, 11

## U, V

ultracrepidarian, 97
utopia, 65
verse, 11
versus, 11
vicuna, 129
vignette, xiii
vulgar, 33
vulgate, 33

## W

waffle, 118
wanderlust, 172
wassail, 29
water, 25
Weltanschauung, 172
werewolf, 29
wild goose chase, 105
woke, 161
wood, 11
wrong, 41

## Y, Z

yam, 158
zeitgeist, 172

## ABOUT THE AUTHOR

Mim Harrison is the author of three other books on the English language (*Wicked Good Words, Smart Words, Words at Work*). Additionally, she has written introductory and prefatory text for books on such masters of language as Samuel Johnson, Cicero, Lincoln, and Robert Louis Stevenson.

As a specialty publisher of limited-edition books, she has collaborated with the Smithsonian, the Library of Congress, the Folger Shakespeare Library, the Morgan Library & Museum, the John F. Kennedy Presidential Library and Museum, and the Churchill Estate.

Harrison is currently an exhibitions editor for The New York Public Library as well as the editorial and brand director of the America the Bilingual project. After studying Latin and French in her school years, she is now learning Spanish.

She and her husband—and their dachshund—divide their time between Florida and Rhode Island.

www.ingramcontent.com/pod-product-compliance
Lightning Source LLC
Chambersburg PA
CBHW060557080526
44585CB00013B/593